THE VIEW FROM THE TURRET

The 743d Tank Battalion during World War II

William B. Folkestad

Foreword William Darien Duncan,
Colonel, U.S.A. (Ret.)

Burd Street Press

This Burd Street Press book
was printed by
Beidel Printing House, Inc.
63 West Burd Street
Shippensburg, PA 17257 USA

In respect for the scholarship contained herein, the acid-free paper in this book meets the guidelines for permanence and durability of the Committee on Production Guidelines for Book Longevity of the Council on Library Resources.

For a complete list of available publications
please write
White Mane Publishing Company, Inc.
P.O. Box 152
Shippensburg, PA 17257 USA

Library of Congress Cataloging-in-Publication Data

Folkestad, William B., 1955–
    The view from the turret : the 743d Tank Battalion during World
War II / William B. Folkestad.
        p.   cm.
    Includes index.
    ISBN 1-57249-001-2. -- ISBN 1-57249-192-2
    1. United States.   Army.   Tank Battalion, 743rd--History.
    2. World War, 1939–1945--Campaigns--Western Front.   3. World War,
    1939–1945--Regimental histories--United States.   I. Title.
    D769.306   743rd.F65   1996
    940.54'1273--dc20

96-2301
CIP

This work is dedicated to Lt. Orlyn H. Folkestad. This work was written for all the children and grandchildren of the men of the 743d.

Table of Contents

Foreword

The author, with his very thorough research, has given credit to the true "warriors" of World War II, the officers and men at and below the combat battalion level. The generals, like Simpson, Bradley and Patton were not the warriors. They were the planners and leaders, but they never engaged in actual combat.

The 743d Tank Battalion, code named "VERIFY," was possibly the most outstanding separate tank battalion in the European Theater. It was fortunate to have supported such famous infantry divisions as the 1st, the 29th, and the 30th (Old Hickory) divisions.

The officers of the 743d Tank Battalion were all products of the University R.O.T.C. (Reserve Officer Training Corps) or 90-day wonders of the O.C.S. (Officers Candidate School). The enlisted men on the other hand were all volunteers or draftees, but they were all great American youth. Their battle cry chosen by the men while the battalion was being formed at Fort Lewis, Washington, was "WE KEEP THE FAITH." All the officers and men who joined the battalion were told that we would keep the Faith our loved ones had in us, our nation had in us, and our God had in us until we defeated the Nazi-Fascist forces.

A majority of the officers and men were from farms and small towns in the midwest. When they joined the battalion they brought with them knowledge of tractors, trucks, and other farm equipment which blended well with the tanks, half-tracks, jeeps and trucks of a tank battalion. Most also had a basic knowledge of guns from their hunting deer, pheasants, ducks, and rabbits. Many had worked in the harvest fields at 110 degrees in Missouri and 20 degrees below zero in Minnesota, the Dakotas, Iowa, Wisconsin, Nebraska, and Michigan. This served them well in the winter combat in the "Battle of the Bulge." Along with this, they brought their Faith which they had learned in their churches, synagogues and at the knees of their parents.

It is only proper that these men of "VERIFY" and their partners be given this honor by the author. It is the privates, corporals, sergeants, and young combat officers who are the "Warriors." They kept the Faith under extremely harsh and hazardous situations.

William Darien Duncan
Colonel U.S.A., rtd.
Former C.O. of the 743d

Preface

In conflicts of any duration and scale, small unit successes are often quickly overshadowed and do not receive their deserved attention. In case of the 743d Tank Battalion, almost nothing is known about one of the most highly decorated tank battalions of World War II. The 743d Tank Battalion was only one small component of the Second World War; nonetheless, its contributions of fifty years ago were very real as was its members' courage and lives. This unit has been largely forgotten by historians and strongly merits acknowledgement of its achievements.

The 743d remains overlooked because of most writers' acceptance of an inherited topical treatment of the events discussed here. For example, on Omaha beach the 743d was the only combat-strength tank battalion supporting both the 1st and the 29th Infantry Divisions; nonetheless its role in aiding those units' efforts to move off the beach have either been completely ignored by historians or minimalized beyond recognition. This trend among historians may be explained by a too heavy (although understandable) reliance upon two official government histories of the Normandy campaign. In the first volume, Taylor's *Omaha Beachhead*, the 743d is mentioned briefly by name and then becomes an anonymous "tank or tanks" without any attempt at an analysis of its role on the battlefield. The second volume, Harrison's *Cross Channel Attack*, relied heavily upon Taylor's work for information on the Omaha front, and the 743d was completely omitted. Consequently, when Cornelius Ryan wrote his historical narrative, *The Longest Day*, the 743d was again overlooked, in part, because of the author's reliance upon previous official histories. The focus of Max Hasting's *Overlord* remained on those topics and units stressed by earlier authors, hence the 743d was again neglected. This adoptive attitude towards previous authors' outlines can be said to characterize the general approach, over the past fifty years, to the battles discussed here.

In the slow-moving engagements of the western European theater of World War II, and against an already taxed yet defiant enemy, it was the men manning Sherman M4 medium tanks who often determined the outcome of violent battlefield encounters, not the tank. The 743d's battlefield experiences provide us with insights into the American use of the Sherman M4 series tank at the battalion level. The battles participated in by the 743d encapsulate and highlight the outstanding heroism associated with the intense and effective use of this inadequate weapon.

The material presented here is personal to the battalion level, the battle within battles, or an objective within the overall strategy. It should however be noted that I have not attempted to portray any battalion except that already mentioned, although the experiences of other tank battalions were oftentimes similar. I would add that the conclusions drawn here are my own. I believe that the history of the 743d is especially useful for examining the problems faced by World War II tank battalions because of the unit's variety of battlefield experiences including amphibious, summer, winter, night, and urban warfare.

This work can be read in two ways. It can be read as a continuous series of battles during which a battalion is constantly adapting weapons and tactics to the reality of the Sherman M4. The chapters can also be read independently as contributions to the histories of several major campaigns.

Tank battalions of World War II were organized and designed to support the infantry to which they were attached. The 743d Tank Battalion was attached briefly to the 29th Infantry Division, followed by permanent attachment to Old Hickory, the 30th Infantry Division. Also temporarily assigned to the 30th Infantry were the 740th (attached December 19, 1944–December 28, 1944) and the 744th (attached February 7, 1945–February 28, 1945) Tank Battalions.

Tank battalions fought under completely different conditions from those of an armored division. A tank battalion could not race ahead of the supporting infantry, nor could a battalion except to exploit and advance into the rear areas of an enemy with massive numbers of tanks. On the contrary, battalion tanks moved quickly only if the infantry moved quickly, and, as was most often the case, they were forced to fight static armored battles against tanks far superior to their own.

My recounting of the 743d begins in June 1944 with "A Beach and a Summer to Remember," a chapter-long discussion of the 743d's decisive role on Omaha beach and the subsequent expansion of the Allied beachhead. This is followed in chapter 2, "The Sherman Medium Tank: On the Front and in the Papers," by an overview of the procurement, design and armor theory behind the development of the Sherman M4. The reader is introduced to the public and press awareness of the difficulties encountered by American armor when matched against its German counterparts (principally through the work of Pulitzer Prize winning journalist Hanson W. Baldwin, war correspondent for the *New York Times*).

Chapter 3, "Seven for Eleven," presents the battalion's introduction to, and mastery of, armored warfare in the Norman *bocage* during the months of July and August 1944. Also included is a brief overview of the 743d's role in the Battle of Mortain.

Another battle in which the 743d has received only partial credit from historians—or less in some cases—is the Battle of the Bulge. Chapter 4, "In a Field near La Glieze, describes the battalion's participation in this crucial battle culminating with the 743d's move to northwestern Germany. This is preceded by a discussion of the battalion's involvement in the Siegfried Line Campaign.

As previously noted, the 743d provides the opportunity to not only historically credit a forgotten battalion, but in addition, to observe the Sherman M4 under a wide variety of battlefield conditions. Therefore, whereas the first three chapters provide detailed examinations of the M4 as it was used by the battalion in amphibious, hedgerow, and winter warfare, chapter 5, "Battles on the Plain of Cologne," introduces the reader to the battalion's problems and experiences with the Sherman medium tank during night combat.

Chapter 6, "On a Street in Magdeburg," begins with the Rhine River crossing and the subsequent expansion by the Allies eastward across the north German countryside to the Elbe River. Chapter 7, "85 Points," summarizes the war's end, the battalion's postwar police duty, and the return stateside of the 743d veterans.

I have made every attempt to maintain the accuracy of the events described here by using original source material such as personal interviews, After-Action Reports, the battalion's S-3 Journals and the unit history compiled in Frankfurt, Germany, at the end of hostilities. To complement this documentation, I have also resorted to contemporary recorded news broadcasts, newspapers, and magazine articles. Finally, I have included secondary historical material whenever an author contributed a unique insight or fact unattainable elsewhere. In preparing this work I have attempted to adhere to the code name of the 743d—"VERIFY!"

A special word needs to be included about the battalion's S-3 Journals compiled from the daily After-Action Reports. The journals are irreplaceable historical documents, for not only do they record factual accounts of daily events but they also supply insight into the joys of achievement and the anguish of disaster and personal loss. The nature of these reports is also interesting. The brief, hurriedly typed pages of June and July 1944 are testimony to battlefield pressures and the less than assured survival of the Allied beachheads. The early reports stand in stark contrast to those of December, and later, when experienced staffs with adequate time furnish fuller battlefield accounts. In fact, these reports are a reflection of the men themselves: hurried and harried in the beginning, they move in the end with a slow swagger suggesting a self assurance born of hard-won success.

Colonel William Darien Duncan, rtd., former commanding officer of the 743d, has offered me much needed information, valuable criticism and correction. Any errors remaining herein are entirely my own. It has been a pleasure to receive Colonel Duncan's carefully typed letters which in their entirety reflect the carbon copies of those documents from fifty years ago with which I have spent so much time. Additional thanks must also be extended to Mr. Charles Brown (Cpl. A Company) who, from the beginning of this project has served me in the best traditions of a S-1, S-2 Liaison Officer combined. To those individuals who have provided their invaluable personal experiences, especial thanks must be addressed: Howard and Lucille Froberg; Joel Matteson; Donald Mason; Dr. Carl Tarlowski; John Shanafelt; Ed Miller; Dr. Ashley Camp; Alvin Tisland; Raymond W. Locke; Joseph Couri, through the courtesy of Mrs. Majorie McCullough; Captain John Roncevich, rtd.; Perry "Cock" Kelly; George Johnson; Jerry Lattimer, Harry Hansen; Tena Jenkins; Tom Snyder; Wendell Henry Jones; Major Joe Harris on behalf of Keith Mayberry, Anthony W. Robinson; John Yocum; Al Westman; Miles Walker; Harlan Whitcomb; Raymond Mullen; Phil Goodridge; William W. McCoy; Orville Jensen; Carroll Banta; Elroy Fournia; Robert Johnson; Gerald Gahl; Chester Johnson; Frank Lancaster; Richard Delfs; Clinton Nodtvedt; Howard Forsberg. Thanks is also made here to Sergeant Major Frederick Friedrich, rtd., who over many cups of coffee patiently explained and interpreted the many intricate details of subjects as varied as armament and tactics to map reading and militareze.

Throughout this project I have been repeatedly impressed by the courtesy of individuals responding to my inquiries. Therefore,

I must also signal my gratitude to James Hall, editor, 823d Tank Destroyer Battalion Newsletter and Frank Towers, 30th Infantry Division Association, "Gator" Chapter. For their assistance in my unsuccessful search for "Andre" I thank Roger Jouet, Secretariat D'Etat Aux Anciens Combattants et Victimes de Guerre and M. Laurence Nain Dit Ducret, Secretariat, TF1, "Perdu de Vue." The research, the interviews, the entire preparation of this manuscript can only be likened to plunging into the passage cut by a now distant vessel. Leaping into the waters every effort is expended to catch up before the wake closes, erasing forever any trace of passage. This brief examination will contribute to keeping the wake cut by the 743d pried wide apart.

The relevant nature of the subject presented here is repeatedly brought to the fore. Who in 1945 would have thought that headlines could be made from a search for Erich Koch's treasure in Weimar, Germany, or from the question of whether or not Rudolf Hess acted alone on May 11, 1941, or indeed that Mussolini's granddaughter would enter the political arena? These and many other "newsworthy items" demonstrate the contemporaneity of the experiences recounted here.

The historian determines the future of the past. It is in sevice to this belief that I write, to help preserve a brief moment in history, contribute to an understanding of the lessons it taught, and honor the men who lived those moments. This goal could never have been realized without the patient support and encouragement of my wife Francine.

I

A Beach and a Summer to Remember

EVEN PEOPLE WHOSE LIVES HAVE BEEN MADE VARIOUS BY LEARNING SOME-
TIMES FIND IT HARD TO KEEP A FAST HOLD ON THEIR HABITUAL VIEWS OF LIFE,
ON THEIR FAITH IN THE INVISIBLE-NAY, ON THE SENSE THAT THEIR PAST JOYS
AND SORROWS ARE A REAL EXPERIENCE, WHEN THEY ARE SUDDENLY TRANS-
PORTED TO A NEW LAND, WHERE THE BEINGS AROUND THEM KNOW NOTHING
OF THEIR HISTORY, AND SHARE NONE OF THEIR IDEAS—WHERE THEIR MOTHER
EARTH SHOWS ANOTHER LAP, AND HUMAN LIFE HAS OTHER FORMS THAN
THOSE ON WHICH THEIR SOULS HAVE BEEN NOURISHED.

George Eliot (1861)

THE ramp dropped like a weighted stage curtain from in front of the three tanks and their crews. In the scene framed by the shadowed sides of the open-topped craft, dark colored obstacles, their bases hidden in the shallow waters, presented a skeletal-like screen to the thick line marking the distant bluffs. Inside the tanks the roar of the engines was only slightly muffled by the radio headsets worn by crew members. With radios switched from Battalion net to intercom the command tank of Charlie Company, 2d Platoon, prepared to leave its wave-tossed tank landing craft (LCT).[1] Crew members listened as the tank commander ordered 28-year-old Alvin Tisland to move out into the wind-driven surf slicing at Omaha beach.

Through the grey, early morning light barely penetrating the hatch-mounted periscope, Tisland strained to identify beach obstacles as his right foot depressed the gas pedal and the left eased out the clutch in smooth, well-practiced movements. With the turn levers held immobile, metal tracks ground the steel decks of the LCT as the 32-ton General Sherman medium tank jerked into motion. Waterproofed hull fittings kept the chillingly cold Channel waters at bay as the descent down the ramp was quickly replaced by the submerged incline of the beach. All along the western half of Omaha beach each successive tank crew copied its leader and moved up to and off the ramps of their LCTs.

Tisland guided his tank out of the waters and over the wide sand flats to a spot below the bluffs. The tank commander opened the turret hatch, surveyed the beach, and yelled excitedly over the intercom, "We're all alone!" On the morning of June 6 the 743d C Company tank was the first American tank to safely land on Omaha beach.

The tanks leaving the LCTs were confronting the object of two years' training, and the focus of everyone's gaze since earliest light. What until now had been an idea divided into eight various sized sectors code-named Fox Red, Fox Green, Easy Red, Easy Green, Dog Red, Dog White, Dog Green, and Charlie, was now a distant dark line marking the horizon and the Norman shoreline. At 0624 under heavy, deadly fire, Charlie Company's amphibious Duplex Drive (DD) tanks unloaded from the LCTs that had brought them from England onto Dog White and Easy Green.[2] Within minutes Baker Company landed on Dog Green, and Able Company followed.[3] Men who had never before seen battle were thrust into sixteen hours of nonstop, lifetaking practice on a beach of a summer to remember.

Omaha beach is four miles long and bordered on either end by two cliffs over 100 feet high. At low tide, wide, hard-packed tidal flats lead upwards from the beach towards a cultivated inland plateau. During high tide the same beach narrows to a few yards in width. Along the western end of the beach the tidal flats merge directly into the sea bluffs. On the eastern end, these same features are separated by narrow marshes. Dog Red at 480 yards was the narrowest beach, whereas the largest, at 3,015 yards, was Fox Red in front of Le Grand Hameau. The 743d's three line companies, in support of the 1st Infantry Division and A Regiment of the 29th Infantry Division, were to attack the five westernmost beaches from Easy Green to Charlie. The plan was for Charlie and Baker Companies in amphibious DD Sherman swimming tanks propelled by twin bronze screws, to launch 4,000 yards from shore and arrive on the beach at H-minus-10. Able Company using waterproofed Sherman wading-tank devices would go into the beach 10 minutes later. A last minute change sent Able Company to all four western beaches, from Dog Green to Easy Green, rather than just Easy

Green and Dog Red.[4] Ideally, the tanks of A, B, and C Companies would array themselves along the water's edge and provide artillery and machine gun cover for the combat engineers scheduled to land 20 minutes before the armor, and for the infantry who would land at H-hour. Under tank protection, the engineers could clear lanes to the beach and then destroy the concrete obstacles blocking the two western beach exits. Six Able Company tanks had been outfitted with dozer blades to aid the engineers. The 743d's objective called for taking the beach, the defenses on the bluffs, and, after pushing southwest, take the nearby town of Isigny where the company was to halt for the night. It would be days before the battalion met its goals.

The only American forces trained with the secret DD tanks in time for the Normandy invasion were the 70th, the 741st, and the 743d Tank Battalions. Of these, the 741st and 743d were to attack on Omaha, but without their light tank companies.[5] Together, these battalions could place nearly 64 medium tanks at the disposal of their attached infantry units.

At H-50, thirty-two 741st DD tanks debarked 6,000 yards off the eastern half of Omaha beach. The 741st tried to swim from distances greater than planned through heavy seas to the safety of the shallower waters covering the tidal flats.[6] Twenty-seven tanks, suffering from sea-inflicted damage to torn canvas, broken struts, and flooded engine compartments, slowly settled to the Channel bottom. Three additional tanks from the 741st's armored assault force, witness to the nearly complete destruction of their battalion, arrived to the tidal flats in an LCT with a jammed ramp.[7]

Because of the early morning tragedy of the 741st, the forces landing on Omaha beach were deprived of nearly half of their allotted armor. The other half, the tanks of the 743d, was saved by an independent last minute decision that brought the tanks to within yards of the tidal flats.

In case of seaborne disaster the men sealed inside the heavily loaded tanks had little opportunity to escape. Some 743d tankers had self-inflating life vests, others wore Davis Life Support Systems that included a respirator. When the driver and assistant driver were wearing either life vest it was impossible to exit their front hatches. To escape a disabled tank both men had to remove their vests and then try to force open their sealed hatch covers. If these efforts failed, the men moved from their lower, forward positions into the turret basket, and escaped out the turret hatch. The passage to safety between the lower and upper compartments depended on the matching of a single opening in the lower part of the turret basket with the back of the forward compartment. This opening was accessible only when the main gun was pointed squarely towards the front. Landing at low tide, one 743d tank crew after another welcomed the reassuring contact of solid ground and their escape from the sensation of floating helplessness.

The carefully planned Omaha timetable was already going astray as naval LCTs brought the first tanks of the 743d onto the tidal flats. Buffeted by winds, LCTs swamped in the cold, surging Channel waters. Some LCTs were misled by naval guide boats, rammed by other vessels, or fell victim to enemy artillery. The LCTs approaching the beach bucked and rolled among the swells. Inside, the tanks gunners waited impatiently until a target, momentarily disappearing behind a white crested wave, reappeared in their sights and a round of 75 mm High Explosive (HE) could be sent beachward. Upon reaching the tidal flats, some LCT ramps failed, or hit uncleared mines. In the churning sea and under enemy fire the LCTs carrying the 743d's three line companies tried to complete the landings according to the general plan. On June 6 only A Company's staff tank reached the beach. Baker Company's staff tank was destroyed in its LCT, whereas Headquarter's staff tank and that of Charlie Company did not come ashore until the afternoon of the seventh.[8]

In the general confusion of the early morning, naval crews landed 743d A and C Company tanks from exits D-1 to E-3 on beaches designated for the 741st Tank Battalion.[9] Here, they joined the remaining DD tanks of the 741st as they began covering the first phase of the assault from where they had been unloaded at the water's edge.

The tanks crawling from their steel motorized boxes advanced through the shallow tidal waters preceded by twin brown watery fans spewing forth from beneath the front fenders. The tankers were not alone on the beach for very long. Men and equipment arriving in 30-minute intervals added to the growing congestion both in and out of the cold waters. Crowded soldiers sought safety behind the same defensive works and beach obstacles the tankers and engineers were seeking to clear. All along the front, fire from the heights decimated incoming craft and soldiers; organization and plan quickly gave way to the pressures of survival and the need to escape the beachfront.

The LCT carrying three C Company DD tanks dropped its ramp. By the time the first tank drove over the ramp and began swimming ashore, the churning engines of the landing craft had been shifted into reverse. One by one the remaining tanks rolled up to the exit, drove off their departing platform, floundered and sank.

The lead tank drove across the beach and stopped; its crew unaware of the fate of their companions. The tank bucked when its gunner, Jerry Lattimer, fired the first round. Targeted by one of the beach guns, an exploding German shell filled the tank with noise and black smoke. Two more rounds from Lattimer's gun brought two more hits that left the tank disabled with three dead crewmen. Despite Lattimer's warnings to stay inside, the tank commander left the turret and began signalling to other tanks for a pick-up when he too was killed. Lattimer later reflected that he then understood why green tankers had been thrown at the German defenses on Omaha. Veteran tankers would have stopped firing after the first hit.[10]

On the beach the 743d discovered that they were in the middle of the cacophony of a building battle. The shrill whistle of incoming artillery seemed to be everywhere, broken only by the rumbling, jarring explosions of detonating shells and the rapid chattering of machine gun fire. The beach was centered between, on the one hand, the naval bombardment passing overhead on its way inland, and on the other hand, the equally fierce bombardment coming from the German shore defenses. On that day it would be proven that each held its dangers.

At 0400 on June 6, Major William D. Duncan roused the men of the 743d's Headquarter staff onboard LCT 29. Those able to eat in the rocking craft swallowed hot coffee and K rations after which equipment and vehicles were checked again in preparation for landing. It was the uneventful beginning of two days of unparalleled bad luck. First, the LCT was prevented from landing on time at H-30 when it was led by a naval guide boat to the wrong assembly location off Omaha beach. Shepherded back to its correct rallying point, the LCT awaited a new time and position among the waves of craft heading to shore. Finally allowed to go in at 0745, LCT 29 was dropping its ramp 200 yards off Dog White Beach when without warning the ramp cables snapped. Unchecked in its downward swing the ramp folded underneath the forward-moving craft, preventing the off-loading of the 743d's command vehicles. At that moment the artillery fire on the beach was so great that offshore observers were confused as to whether the bombardment was friendly or enemy.[11] Unable to unload and unwilling to abandon the battalion's much needed equipment, the crew guided their disabled craft 1,000 yards out into the Channel to seek help. After two frustrating hours of unsuccessful attempts to obtain aid, the naval lieutenant commanding the LCT decided to retry landing the vehicles in its hold. Before progressing very far, they were again halted, this time because the navy was preparing to shell the beach.[12]

Thick cloud cover met the Allied airmen seeking the German defenses at Omaha, and so the bombs designated for the beach were dumped inland. In the words of one battalion veteran the bluffs "should have been ploughed," instead lush green grass waved slowly in the sea breeze.[13] The job of breaking through the German beach defenses became an arduous day-long task. Now continuous fire from the Germans' concrete bunkers, concealing artillery, mortars, and no less than 35 rocket launching sites, were churning the sands of the four-mile long beach. In the tunnels and zigzag slit trenches crisscrossing the heights overlooking the beach, men and their supplies moved relatively freely from one defensive point to the next; repeatedly reoccupying positions that the attackers thought they had overcome.

The Germans' heavy defensive fire was taking its toll on the invaders. Thirty minutes into H-Hour, four 743d DD tanks on Easy Red were supporting, what was later estimated to be, fewer than 100 fighting men.[14]

Baker Company's ungainly, and unlikely, DD tanks swam in from the outer limits of the tidal flats opposite Dog Green beach. Twin bronze screws slowly pushed the tanks the last few hundred yards through the surf until their tracks could claw at the dun-colored sandy bottom.

Corporal Fawcett pressed his forehead against the hatch-mounted periscope while watching the jagged steel stakes marking the tidal defenses grow larger. In the distance, Fawcett recognized the church steeple towering above Vierville-sur-Mer from the black and white reconnaissance photos studied in England. Suddenly, the tank jerked to a stop. Exchanged glances communicated the shared thought that the engine compartment had flooded, leaving the tank powerless. But behind him, even with his radio headgear on, Fawcett could hear the noise of the engine, and everyone could feel the vibrations of the twin screws. Fawcett removed his radio headset and announced he would investigate. The driver disengaged the props as Fawcett climbed over the canvas curtain surrounding the upper hull and splashed into the cold Channel waters. Inside, the silent crew listened to the sounds of the battle carried on the cool sea-scented air invading the tank hull through Fawcett's open hatch. The thunder of exploding artillery seemed to be everywhere, but somewhere, outside in the distance, machine guns could be heard and closer still, occasional ricochets, as bullets deflected upwards from the water's surface.

Fawcett's tank had left its LCT 200 yards from what was believed to be the outer limit of the first line of the German coastal defenses. Fawcett groped under the tank in the dark sand-filled waters until he discovered that the hull had snagged on one of the mined metal tetrahedrons made from steel rails, now barely covered by an outgoing tide. Fawcett resurfaced and quickly explained that the tank they had brought from England was helpless. When the tide would be out, the tank would fall from its floating perch and most likely end up on its side. In the meantime, the tank was not only useless, but immobile and, therefore, very dangerous to sit in. The tank commander ordered the abandonment of the vehicle, and the remainder of the crew climbed onto the deck of the gently rocking tank. But as his friends pushed down the torn canvas curtain and began dropping over the side, Fawcett reentered the turret and destroyed the radio. Afterwards, he too reemerged into the smoky grey light of dawn and swam away from the silent tank towards the noises of a building battle.[15]

When the D-Day flotilla started on its 100-mile journey to the Norman coast, the battalion's tank-filled LCTs departed the staging area off the coast of England under strict radio silence. The tanks in their little crafts were part of an enormous armada, but the throbbing engines of the LCTs seemed louder than noises from troop-filled ships, so that nearby huge dark hulks seemed to be slipping silently over the water.

When the engine of the LCT carrying Harry Hansen and four C Company tanks failed, the craft coasted to a rolling stop. On the passing ships helmet-shadowed faces leered silently or threw out unheard but imaginable taunts. The armada bypassed the lonely craft wallowing in the outrushing Channel waters.

Under the ban of radio silence the unfaithful engine was finally restarted and the question passed among the men was, "Which way to France?" When a fisherman pointed the naval crew in the general direction, the LCT set out, hoping to make up for lost time.

After being under way for what seemed to be too long, and apparently alone in the Channel waters, the decision was made to break radio silence. The radio introduced the isolated group to the invasion battle, broadcasting the fearfilled, frantic call of someone demanding to be taken off the beach. Within a short time the fisherman's directions proved correct, the LCT re-entered the armada and continued headlong into the fight.[16]

Tank commanders sought to weave a way for their tanks through the deadly maze of mined, wooden and steel beach obstacles. At a little past H-hour, eight LCTs carrying 743d A Company tanks arrived off Easy Green and Dog Red, the two beaches bracketing Exit D-3. Two tanks had been lost on the way in, three more were hit and put out of action on the beach. The contingent included eight tank dozers towing trailers, some loaded with explosives for the engineers. Other trailers carried dark-colored crates filled with extra rounds for the tankers' 75 mm main gun. Although the move across the flats to the foot of the bluffs would be a slow dangerous task, A Company, the last of the 743d's line companies to land, was present on nearly all the western beaches.[17]

The tanks of 1st Platoon, Able Company, quickly discovered that cleared lanes were not yet at hand, and between them and the rest of the battalion were uncleared beach obstacles and a minefield. In the distance, across the flats in front of exit D-1, C Company's DD tanks and eight B Company tanks dueled with the enemy beach fortifications placing flanking fire on the Dog Beaches. Large white numbers painted on the tanks' broad canvas exhaust stacks marked their every movement.[18]

George Johnson watched through his periscope as his A Company tank advanced towards the mined, metal rails planted deep in the hard-packed sand. In the thick glass of the rectangular prism he saw the neighboring obstacles where men, in dark, water-soaked uniforms, sought safety. When the dozer blade collided with the metal rails, the force of the exploding *Tellermine* violently shook the air, tank, and crew, blanketing the area with water, smoke and debris. At first the tank commander thought that the painful stinging on his face was from shrapnel instead of the mud that had splattered him and his tank.[19] The effect of the blast on soldiers around the tank was unknown.

As the tank churned through the surf, its commander, Staff Sergeant Floyd Jenkins, realized the hopelessness of blindly blundering through the German defenses. Jenkins crawled out of the turret, moved to the side of the hull, and leapt into the shallow waters. Exposed to the withering fire being laid on the beach by its defenders, Jenkins struggled to keep upright in the waves as his tanker's coveralls became heavy with the cold Channel waters. With slow, exaggerated movements calculated to withstand the outrushing water, or braced against an incoming wave, Jenkins sought tank-width alleys through the shoulder high, mined hurdles. Lost to the surrounding battle, the five tanks crawled in low gear to the speed of one wading individual as they wove their way up and across the tidal flats. Upon reaching the last rows of obstacles and benefiting from the ruinous evidence everywhere present of those who had already passed, Jenkins led his platoon across the mine field. One by one the tanks drove across the brown sandy waste and deployed on the far side. Still unharmed, Jenkins clambered back up and into the relative safety of his turret.[20] Farther down the beach, Captain Vodra Philips, A Company commander, also dismounted to lead his tanks afoot.

The LCT carrying A Company's 3d Platoon tanks bumped onto the submerged bank marking the tidal flats. Inside Tank 13 gunner Don Mason felt the waterproofed Sherman drive off the ramp and settle lazily into the water. Fear and doubt mounted among the crew as the tank continued settling and the Channel waters reaching the turret began pouring through the open hatch. With the memories of training accidents—barely 16 days before—still fresh in his mind Mason rose from his seat beside the main gun. At that moment the tracks grabbed at the bottom and the tank began crawling upwards towards shallower waters.[21]

After weaving slowly through mined obstacles that reminded Mason of gigantic children's jacks, the tank stopped before the road-topped sea wall. All along the seaward side of the bank Mason saw prone, water-soaked soldiers. The tank commander, Sergeant Orlyn Folkestad, ordered Mason to drive along the promenade and look for a slope free of men to use as a route to the road top. Unsuccessful in their search, Mason asked on the tank intercom, "Why won't these guys move to let us pass?" "Because they're all dead," the tank commander replied.[22]

A tall, slight man with glasses jumped from an LST and momentarily sank from view under the water. Carl Tarlowski, the 743d's doctor, ignored the initial shock of the cold and wet as he struggled and pushed with his legs against the heavy water. The quiet practice of a pediatrician seemed a vague nearly forgotten dream. Tarlowski began organizing aid and administering to the seemingly endless casualties; it would be three days before he would again wear dry clothing. He moved to the men huddled behind the protection of the sea wall, and was suddenly aware that everything was wrong. The battalion's doctor knelt beside first one soldier and then another; men were identified who needed immediate evacuation and others who would never leave Omaha.[23] Someone, somewhere, mentioned that the battalion's commander, Colonel Upham, had been hit and needed attention. But Colonel Upham was lost on a beach littered with wounded.

For over a year, Colonel Upham had trained the 743d for just this moment. But Normandy was a long way from the firing ranges of Fort Lewis, Washington, and completely unlike the April practice landings at Slapton Sands in England. At first unable to land, Colonel Upham directed his battalion by radio from his LCT. When finally able to make the beach, Upham moved on foot from tank to tank organizing defensive fire and infantry support, even after his right shoulder took a sniper's bullet. Upham stayed with his men and continued to coordinate fire and direct his tanks until early in the afternoon when the first indications of a possible exit from the beach became thinkable. At that point, A Company commander, Captain Vodra Philips, assumed field command of the battalion until Major William Duncan arrived the following day.[24]

Howard Froberg, a spare blue-eyed Minnesotan farmboy, pressed his forehead against the periscope mount. In the view framed by the rectangular-shaped lense, he could easily make out the mine-tipped, steel beach obstacles. Above, on the distant blufftops could be seen scurrying, small, grey uniformed figures. Suddenly a bullet shattered the thick glass outer lens. Froberg jerked the scope from its mount and tried to force another into its place. Unsuccessful in his attempts, Froberg unfastened his seatbelt and strained upwards with his arms against the grip of the waterproofing material sealing the hatch. The hatch swung open and cool sea air displaced the warm stale atmosphere of the gloomy interior. Froberg's slim frame popped up and down through the hatch for the rest of the day as he guided the tank along the beachfront.

A testimony to both the quality and training of the men of the 743d is found in how rapidly crewmen replaced seriously wounded or killed officers. In some instances tank crews took in men from disabled tanks. Frank Lancaster of B Company had just made it to the beach when his tank was knocked out. The crew dispersed, seeking positions in nearby tanks. Lancaster fought with A Company for two weeks until a replacement tank was available.[25]

Farther along the beach Jenkins had now taken over command of A Company's 1st Platoon after his commanding officer was killed. Other line company sergeants did likewise as crew members shuffled positions to keep their tanks fighting. Everywhere, 743d tank commanders, and later their replacements, kept their turret hatches open as bullets splattered or ricocheted across the hard metal surfaces.

All morning incoming artillery rounds exploded on the beach and in the sea, sending funnels of water and brown sand skywards that in turn cascaded over the men and lumbering tanks. To the tank crews isolated from the showers of sand and shrapnel it quickly became obvious from the sound, shock waves, and ground tremors, how near a miss had been. The ineffectiveness of the airstrike was sorely felt and limited the ability of the armor to deal with their preassigned targets. Once on the beach, tankers became preoccupied with the strongpoints in front of their landing areas and had to temporarily abandon designated targets.[26] Throughout the entire day, only one, lone, P-38 appeared, strafed the beachfront and departed.[27]

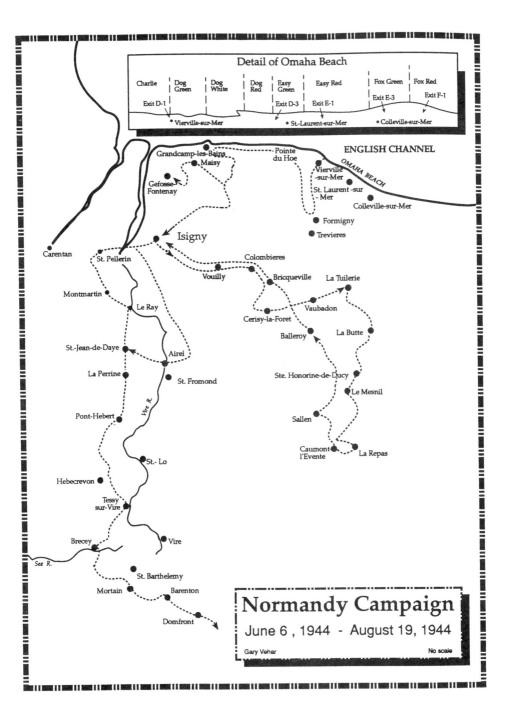

Detail of Omaha Beach

| Charlie | Dog Green | Dog White | Dog Red | Easy Green | Easy Red | Fox Green | Fox Red |

Exit D-1   Exit D-3   Exit E-1   Exit E-3   Exit F-1

• Vierville-sur-Mer   • St-Laurent-sur-Mer   • Colleville-sur-Mer

ENGLISH CHANNEL

Grandcamp-les-Bains
• Maisy
Pointe du Hoe
Gefosse-Fontenay
OMAHA BEACH
Vierville-sur-Mer
St. Laurent -sur - Mer
Colleville-sur-Mer

Carentan
Isigny
Formigny
Trevieres

St. Pellerin
Colombieres
Vouilly
Bricqueville
La Tuilerie

Montmartin
Le Ray
Vaubadon
Cerisy-la-Foret
Balleroy
La Butte

St.-Jean-de-Daye
Airel
Ste. Honorine-de-Ducy

La Perrine
St. Fromond
Le Mesnil

Pont-Hebert
Vire R.
Sallen

St.- Lo
Caumont l'Evente
La Repas

Hebecrevon

Tessy sur-Vire

Brecey
Vire

See R.
St. Barthelemy

Mortain
Barenton

Domfront

Normandy Campaign
June 6 , 1944 - August 19, 1944

Gary Vehar   No scale

John Parsons, a C Company tank commander, had just engaged his tank in its mission on the beach when a mine tore into its tracks, rendering it useless. Parsons hardly needed to give the abandon order; the explosion shook the tank with such force that everyone knew what to do and the quickest way to do it. Parsons made his way to a nearby A Company dozer. Forward German bunkers rained down medium artillery and plenty of machine gun fire on the lone tank, thwarting their efforts to destroy the hardened concrete barrier blocking the beach exit. The struggle unexpectedly turned in favor of the attackers when a French battleship purposely grounded itself offshore and began laying continuous fire onto the defenses dug into the bluff. Seizing the opportunity, Parsons and his newly adopted crew began using the rear deck of their dozer to haul dynamite from the torn hull of a nearby barge. In all, several tons of explosives were used to reduce the concrete mass to manageable proportions.[28]

For the men of the 743d the battle of Omaha was more than individual survival or the winning of a beach. With exits blocked and the assault faltering, the battle of June 6 became a desperate bid for the survival of a tank battalion's line companies. From a German observation point above the bluffs the situation on the beach must have seemed absolutely hopeless. Early in the morning, only two hours into the landings, a forward observer for the German 352d Division reported that the Americans' assault on Omaha had halted.[29] That very same moment at six or more locations along the front, men were penetrating the heights overlooking the beach.[30] Between 0800 and 0900 another 600 troops, primarily the 2d Ranger Battalion, made it off Dog White beach.[31]

Nearby at Easy Green members of the 3d Battalion, 116th Infantry, had also made it over the top alongside Colonel Canham, their commander.[32] Two 743d tankers were with them. On D-Day minus 2 Wendell Jones had been assigned as liaison officer between 743d tanks and the 116th Infantry along with Jean Blanchette, a French Canadian. Jones and Blanchette landed in the first wave, lugging their 85-pound radio up and over slippery sandy embankments, hurriedly following the colonel wherever he went. Whenever the infantry or tanks were unable to overcome beach defenses, the two tankers radioed fire requests to Major Duncan in the command half-track aboard LCT 29. From there, the calls were forwarded to naval gunners.

By midmorning C Company of the 116th Infantry and the 5th Ranger Battalion had forced their way through exits D-1, and D-3, in front of Les Moulins, aided by the 743d's A and C Company tanks.[33] Shortly after landing, E Company penetrated Easy Red followed by G Company of the 116th Infantry between E-1 and E-3 draws.[34] Despite these small successes penetrations inland continued to be a slow and painful affair. On the bluffs the soldiers starting to confront and harass the German defenders found their actions limited by the loss of their officers and specialized equipment, poor communications, mixed-up units and scattered headquarter groups.[35] Extensive defensive works, terrain, and the continual bombardment of the beach hampered the reinforcement of the isolated groups fighting on the blufftops.

Across the front, smoke and dust from naval bombardments hung in an air damp with an early morning mist. The dust cloud draping the beaches made identification of landing areas, already a difficult enough task in the rough seas, even more difficult for naval control vessels. And as the day wore on, changing tidal currents added to the confusion by pushing landing craft east of their target points.[36]

Naval forward observers knew that a German artillery battery, operating somewhere behind the center of Dog Green Beach, was continually knocking out LCTs, making the advance to the beach difficult if not impossible in some instances. At 0900 the order was given to find and silence it, but like the inland batteries at nearby Maisy, an enormous naval bombardment was necessary before the target was subdued.[37]

By midmorning the wreckage of abandoned vehicles and naval transport vessels dotted the water's edge. To the left of C Company tanks, the combined actions of the tide and waves had pushed the stern of an abandoned naval craft around so that it lay on its side parallel to the beach. A lone figure, too far away to identify, emerged near a davit jutting skyward above the waves. The figure fastened a line to the support and hung himself.[38]

Just before noon, 5th Battalion Rangers entered Vierville-sur-Mer where they were later joined by 1st Platoon, Company B of the 116th Infantry. This group dug in at the chateau located near the village main road and held off German troops being trucked up to reinforce the seaside village. Inadequate communications limited operations. In fact, it was soon discovered that the only radio in the Vierville area was that of Blanchette and Jones, the 743d's liaison officer.[39] While the battle for the village of Vierville raged on, the exit behind them remained closed.

On Dog Green, 743d B Company tanks fought their way onto the elevated gravel causeway leading to Vierville-sur-Mer. The tanks slowly advanced, stopping to occasionally fire as they tried to force their way up to the exit. Unbeknownst to the tankers, observers on the destroyer *Carmick* were closely watching where the tank rounds landed. The *Carmick* gunners used the bursts of the tankers' 75 mm to correct their aim onto the same bluff locations.[40] Shortly afterwards, the tanks pulled back, and for about an hour the battleship *Texas* shelled exit D-1 leading into Vierville and exit D-3 in front of Les Moulins.[41] During the bombardment the steeple of Vierville's church, a landmark for incoming craft, was destroyed.[42]

Farther east, A Company's dozers completed cutting a route up the western slopes of the draw leading to Saint-Laurent. Upon arriving on the plateau the open fields of fire limited further penetration inland, causing beach traffic to become dangerously jammed on the new road.[43]

Down on the beach the noise outside the tanks was deafening. Inside, cannoneers and their assistant gunners responded to their tank commanders' radio instructions as rounds placed in the breach were sent on their way. Cannoneers jerked fresh shells from the ready racks. With each round fired, the tanks bumped back on their tracks while inside a sharp metallic ring sounded out as hot brass casings dropped from breaches onto metal floors. Without the benefit of forward observers and unable to see well in the haze-enveloped beach, tank commanders strained to determine from where incoming rounds originated, and directed their gunners to shoot accordingly. While on the beach the tankers fired an average of 100 rounds, but crews soon discovered that special concrete-busting shells were of little use, and that their return fire was imprecise and with limited effect, as had been observed from the Carmick.

Tanks were valuable when clearing obstacles, but efforts to gain control of an exit were slowed by the increased enemy fire directed at approaching armor. During battle, distant cries for assistance were inaudible over the noise of tracks, engines, guns and radios. Few infantrymen were willing to expose themselves to enemy gunfire to make personal contact with tank crews. It was later determined that the best coordination between tanks and infantry was obtained on Fox Green beach in front of Colleville-sur-Mer.[44] In the opinion of the commander of the 2d Battalion, 116th Infantry, the tanks "saved the day."[45]

Unable to move out in front of the infantry, the armor remained tactically paralyzed on the beachfront bordering the lower bluffs. While maneuvering along the bluff bottom, drivers gave special attention to the V-shaped, fifteen-foot deep tank ditch. Many took advantage of those areas destroyed or filled in during the day by dozers or artillery. Other sections of the ditch, filled with the water-soaked wounded and the fearful, remained impassable.

As the morning hours progressed, another attack was made on the tanks. Waves of the incoming tide began lapping at the hull sides, limiting how the tanks maneuvered as they tried to support the infantry. Met in the early morning by wide, brown sandy beaches, B and C Companies later moved to Dog Red to avoid being engulfed by the midday tide covering one hundred yards of beach every hour.[46] As the cold Channel waters advanced, wounded men huddled close to the beach wall or clung to beach obstacles. High tide also forced the tanks against the bluffs where, lacking room to maneuver, they became oversized ducks in a German shooting gallery.

President Roosevelt announced the invasion mid-morning on the east coast of the United States; noon on the beach. At about the same time as the president's address the commanding officer of the German 352d felt justified in the optimistic early morning report of a faltered invasion and diverted some of his forces eastward to strengthen the sector under attack by the British.[47] But down on the beach the three line companies of the 743d were still embroiled in battle.

Operable tanks moved with the tide, around and at times over the dead and wounded littering the beach. Without air support and under overwhelming incoming fire from the bluffs, tank commanders left their turret hatches open, exposing themselves to better direct their gunners firing over the slopes onto the plateau.[48] Everyone was subject to the 155 mm and 88 mm rounds ranged in on the beach along with heavy automatic weapon fire. Some 85 machine gun nests facing the beach and others flanking the draws leading to the bluffs rained continual fire onto the attackers.[49] Also dropping like rain on the attackers were the mortars fired from well prepared bunkers equipped with the ranges of important targets painted on the concrete rims of their pits.[50]

Shortly after midday, troops[51] gained the high ground at exits D-3 and E-1 just as two destroyers came within 1,000 yards of Les Moulins and began firing onto the German positions located there. Someone perceived an opportunity to escape through the D-3 draw, and orders were given for operable 741st tanks to make for the exit—of the three that arrived, two were knocked out in the draw by mines.[52] Farther up the draw, the advance became bottlenecked in front of Saint-Laurent-sur-Mer, the small village commanding the high ground at the head of exit E-1. The congestion resulted from a lack of hedgerows in the fields around the exit that could conceal flanking movements across the open ground. In an attempt to relieve the exit, an attack was made on Saint-Laurent but this was broken off when the GIs were hit by friendly naval gunfire.

Weakened and shaken, the troops moved south of the town for the night.[53] Prevented in their attempt to escape, the remaining tank of the 741st drove down the beach to just west of exit D-3 and gained the heights using the road cut earlier in the day by the 743d.[54]

With the return of the low afternoon tide engineers again worked to destroy re-exposed beach obstacles and by evening nine more lanes were added to the four that had been opened and marked during the morning.[55] Work on the beach minefields and particularly the exits continued into the night. But even days later, vessels could only access Omaha through limited cleared channels.[56]

By late afternoon, exit E-3 at the eastern end of the beach was open and handling traffic. The 745th Tank Battalion landed here, at 1630 and moved to a night bivouac on the bluff top, losing only three tanks to mines.[57] In one of the many ironies of the day, 743d tanks, beach-bound since early dawn, were still confined to the western end of the Omaha shoreline.

In the late afternoon German artillery directed on the beaches from Easy Green towards Vierville increased. At about the same time the "D-3 open-draw rumor" spread to some of the 743d tankers.[58] However, the tankers backed away upon arrival when they discovered that attempts were still being made to clear it, and the appearance of more tanks only drew more German fire. Forced to make the difficult return among the beach dead and wounded, it was discovered that combat engineers had reopened exit D-1 after it had been opened and then reclosed by rubble shifted by naval fire.[59] Opened to limited traffic at 1700, it would be another four and a half hours before B Company tanks became the first elements of the 743d to move off the beach towards the smoking rubble that had been Vierville-sur-Mer.[60] One hour later A Company followed, with C Company arriving at 2230 hours.[61] Farther east, 17 additional tanks exited E-1 and joined with the 116th's 3d Battalion in blocking the coastal highway at Le-Grand-Hameau behind Fox Red beach.[62]

Stranded offshore in their damaged LCT, the 743d's Headquarters group had escaped another disaster. Midafternoon, a passing vessel cut LCT 29's anchor cable, ramming the craft and punching a hole in its side. As the landings continued in the approaching darkness, the apprehensive, sea-weary group tied themselves to a troop landing craft (LST), for the night.

With the aid of accompanying tanks to blow away remaining obstacles, forces landed in the morning, and those still arriving, moved slowly up through the gully exits bordered on either side by bushes smoldering from battle-caused fires. Only the unpredictable, jarringly loud bursts and brilliant orange flashes of enemy artillery dropping on beach exits slowed the men and machines moving up the draws. Off the beach those in front sorely felt the lack of specialized equipment as men substituted life and limb to locate mines.

All along Omaha, machine gun fire with heavy sniping continued until the end of the day with the beach remaining under artillery fire throughout the evening. At Vierville-sur-Mer the 743d's Charlie and Baker Companies consolidated their positions and made contact with their pre-assigned infantry regiments.[63]

At the end of sixteen hours of fighting to escape the beach, C Company had had one tank disabled by a fire when still in its LCT, two were lost to rough seas, and another was lost on the beach;[64] Baker Company had lost seven tanks,[65] and Able Company had only eight tanks of its initial sixteen tanks and six dozers.[66] During the first days' fighting on Omaha, V Corps lost an estimated 50 tanks destroyed or disabled and 3,000 men killed, wounded or missing in action.[67] Despite these expenditures of men and equipment, the deepest inland penetrations were limited to 1,500 to 2,000 yards, mainly around Colleville.[68] Over the next few days the immediate goal was to provide for the maximum landing of much needed supplies and reinforcements by pushing inland and forcing the German artillery out of range of the beach.

Under the low cast early morning light of June 7, tank crews stirred from fitful naps. In the cool morning air the normally pleasant humid smell of the Channel was now mixed with the heavier odor of burned grass, mouldering dwellings, and the dank odor of sweat-bathed companions. As dawn brightened their surroundings, those lucky enough to possess C rations heated them over the sputtering blue flames of portable Coleman burners. Slowly, all around Vierville the dark, unfamiliar, almost fluid shapes that had been enveloped by the night hardened into green trees, fire-blackened houses, men and tanks. American expectations of a night attack had not become reality, primarily because the Germans' 352d, that had stubbornly fought the advances of the Omaha landing, was the very force that was to have been used for a counterattack.[69]

Jones and Blanchette were nearby, still with Colonel Canham. Jones recalled that night had brought time for reflection, "As long as you were doing something and moving you didn't notice fear, but as soon as you stopped is when things started welling up inside you—that's when you started getting scared."[70] The exhausting ordeal had taken the last of his strength. Unable to rest, Jones had passed the night taking naps while leaning against a tree.

The brief rest, taken in and under tanks, had provided little in the way of a respite. But as the surrounding countryside revealed itself to the tankers the still vivid sensations obtained on the beach submerged beneath the awareness of survival and the prospect of expanding their hard won, but precarious toehold. Outside the tanks, crews performed quick maintenance checks while, inside, remaining rounds were counted as the lingering odors of cordite and sweat were quickly disguised by the smell of cigarette smoke. The raking light of dawn revealed that the ground around the tanks was littered with the dead of the previous day. These were for the most part ignored until an individual's desire for a souvenir overcame the instinctive inviolability of death.

Daylight also brought a return of German sharpshooters. Enemy snipers became the plague of tank commanders exposed in their turrets and the invisible roadblock halting drivers delivering supplies and infantry sweeping mines. Located in trees, ruined houses and churches a round of tank HE was often required to silence their operations.

On the morning of June 7 the coastal road from Saint-Laurent to Vierville was still so hot that the beach was used for transit between exits D-1 and D-3.[71] Among the tankers a share and make-do attitude prevailed until the fuel and ammo starting to arrive on the beach would become available. Some A Company men took advantage of the early morning low tide to return to the beach and salvage two amphibious trucks (DUWKS), a tank and a dozer abandoned the previous day by their crews.

Still dangerous, the beach of June 7 presented a face completely unlike that of the previous morning. Tides had deposited the smaller debris in a long thick line marking the limits of high water. Cast-off and lost equipment from ammunition to personal gear were jumbled together. Wounded men still clung to life among the beach obstacles, burned vehicles, abandoned craft and swamped or sunken barges. Higher still, long rows of dead covered by blankets awaited evacuation, as did those that were as yet, uncollected. Organization of the beach would take days, and during that time the erratic sniping and unpredictable explosions of German mines and artillery punctuated the various beach activities.

Around midmorning the pace at Vierville began to quicken. The Germans tried a small counterattack followed by heavy shelling from Trevieres and a company-strength counterattack from the south that forced its way past the chateau (where counterattacks had been held the previous day) before being stopped by rifle and mortar fire.[72] In response to the threat of further attacks concentrated on Vierville, 743d tanks began a series of missions aimed at consolidating the surrounding territory and relieving other D-Day forces.

Caught between the beach and the dark forms of the ships farther offshore, Headquarters staff had been forced by this time to abandon LCT 29 and had climbed aboard the LST to which they had been tied overnight. After their transfer the sinking craft was taken at high tide through one of the cleared lanes and beached. But the bad luck of LCT 29 was not yet over. While beaching the wreck, the accompanying naval craft detonated a mine, killing one sailor and injuring another. When the crew was maneuvering to return to its offshore position they were struck by machine gun and 88 mm artillery fire.

Meanwhile, Headquarters unloaded into a DUWK which they quickly abandoned due to a rudder problem. That afternoon the men from LCT 29 transferred a third time when they climbed aboard a passing LCM and landed 15 yards offshore. The sea-weary group jumped into the shallow waters, waded ashore, and moved down the beach to where naval personnel were unloading Headquarter vehicles from the wrecked LCT. Duncan assumed command of the battalion and gave instructions to those still on the beach concerning the recovery of much needed equipment. Thinking to immediately rejoin the battalion's line companies, the men from Headquarters exited at D-3 below Saint-Laurent-sur-Mer but were advised not to go farther because of the stiff enemy resistance around Vierville.[73] On June 8, Major Duncan departed Colleville in his command half-track with a platoon of tanks for Maisy, but was stopped at Grandcamps-les-Bains by bomb craters and darkness. Within days Major Duncan was officially designated as 743d Battalion commander and was given a battlefield promotion to Lieutenant Colonel. Over the next eleven months, Duncan successfully brought the battalion to the banks of the Elbe River.

One of the Vierville forces' immediate objectives was the relief of the Rangers surrounded at Pointe-du-Hoe.[74] Although the Rangers' positions were within sight of the Vierville bluffs it was two days before a task force using 743d tanks joined them.[75] The relief group started out on June 8 when two platoons of B Company tanks with infantry pushed down the narrow coastal road connecting Point-du-Hoe and Vierville. The group sought to advance by sheer force along the hard-surfaced tree-lined road bordering the shell-pitted terrain of the Pointe, bypassing enemy positions or spraying them with machine gun fire. Upon reaching Saint-Pierre-du-Mont, near the exit road to Pointe-du-Hoe, enemy artillery forced the tanks to withdraw. The tanks reformed at Saint-Pierre and that afternoon they tried once again to push past the exit road but this time the infantry got caught by enemy artillery and the attack was halted.

On the 9th, a third attempt to break through to the Ranger position was organized. This time the 5th Rangers and 1st Battalion, 116th Infantry, moved across country from Saint-Pierre-du-Mont to the Pointe. At the same time, the 3d Battalion, 116th Infantry, and a platoon of 743d tanks attacked from the south and southwest towards the Rangers. During the ensuing battle the destroyer *Ellyson* fired 140 rounds onto nearby German positions. Within a short time the vanguard of the task force reached the Rangers. But in the push to the Pointe the second force lost three tanks to mines. The remaining tanks, hampered by poor communications and confused by the Rangers' use of captured German weapons, started firing on the Pointe and nearby German troops to the west, causing additional Ranger casualties.[76]

While the attacks on the Pointe were under way, other battalion tankers drove farther south in an attempt to link up with American forces from Utah beach. As part of this action C Company tanks and infantry attacked the German strongpoint at Grandcamp.[77] After one tank was lost to a mine the undestroyed beach road bridge was taken and secured. The Grandcamp attack had been coordinated with another from the south, but the latter force stopped just short of their objective when the tanks ran out of fuel.[78] In the ensuing days, additional attacks were made towards Maisy, Gefosse and Fontenay although supply from the beach remained a problem.[79] Even on June 8 the Omaha landing area remained under fire from the battered German artillery position at Trevieres.

The battalion tanks pushed southwest from the Omaha beachhead amid evidence of the American air assault. Broken aircraft and abandoned supplies dotted the landscape and, in the afternoon sea breeze, parachutes shivering with life hovered over the heavy motionless bodies still in their harnesses.

In the course of the next two weeks the battalion line companies and troops from the 115th and 116th Infantry Regiments of the 29th Infantry Division pushed back the German defenders through the Norman farmlands, hedgerows and orchards. The Germans hotly contested every cluster of homes, overgrown field boundary, and road junction. As the defensive line was rolled back, German artillery and mortar barrages replaced direct fire. Numerous mine fields also blanketed the countryside, plaguing advances and flanking movements by tanks and accompanying troops. When struck by a tank, tracks and parts of suspension systems could be blown off or severely damaged. Tank crews evacuating their disabled vehicles, fell prey to the equally numerous antipersonnel mines sowed along the roadsides and in ditches.

Mines kept crews' nerves on edge throughout the upcoming months. A mine detonated to the outside of a track could disable the tank, but generally left the crew unharmed. A mine detonating between the tracks could produce devastating results. In such instances the tracks contained the detonation, channelling the force of the explosion upwards through the escape hatch underneath the assistant driver's seat, filling the interior with hot black smoke. If the turret hatch was closed, the force of the blast smashed the commander against the turret ceiling. The battalion operated throughout the war without adequate mine-clearing equipment, never knowing when the sudden unexpected explosion of a mine would disable or kill.

In the early weeks of June, and during the months to come, night brought an uncertain calm to the battlefront. Attacks were broken off, lines consolidated, and tanks positioned themselves to provide one another with covering fields of fire. The June skies were often overcast, making the nights seem darker and the temperature cooler. As the last of the wounded were evacuated from the forward outposts, C rations were eaten and tanks refueled and rearmed. Nighttime also diminished the allied monopoly on Norman airspace, and German air missions nicknamed "Bedcheck Charlie" became a regular event.[80] Although generally ineffective, they could not be ignored. Overflights dropping flares accompanied by a few bombs meant a photo reconnaissance flight had passed overhead. In such instances the tankers changed their bivouac locations. Early dawn sometimes brought German dive bombers, an unwelcome and deadly interruption thankfully limited by the rapidly expanding light of a new day.

After achieving the north-south linkage between Allied beachheads, the push east and inland continued. Behind Omaha, elements of the 29th, 1st, and 2d Divisions with tanks of the 743d, extended the beachhead into the high ground of Cerisy-la-Foret, an area within artillery range of Omaha.[81] The forest consisted then, as it does today, of narrowly spaced trees, with tall thin trunks supporting high foliage that darkens the underbrush like an umbrella. The drive eastward did not stop at the forest edge. The objective was Caumont-l'Evente, a small village sited on a low hill only 750 feet above sea level, yet commanding a view of the upper Drone valley and of the German line of communications from Caen to Saint-Lo and the Vire, in the Avranches region.[82]

On the morning of June 12 a small force consisting of Company F, 2d Battalion, 29th Infantry, with 743d C Company tanks leading the way cleaned out Caumont by 0900.[83] Twelve miles inland, Caumont remained the deepest push into the German-held Norman countryside until the Allies' July offensive.[84] With Caumont in American hands, Omaha beach was free of enemy bombardment.

Characteristic of the tankers' experience thus far, the attack on Caumont had met little armored resistance. Although the 2d Panzer Division arrived in the area on the 11th, it lacked heavy antitank guns, tanks and artillery, and en route had suffered heavy losses to air attack. Also bordering the Omaha beachhead was Battlegroup Heintz, a mix of the 17th SS Panzer Grenadier Division, the remainder of the 352d Division, and 2 engineer and infantry battalions. These forces were thinly stretched from Montmartin En-Graignes to the western end of the Vire-Taut Canal.[85]

Following their success at Caumont, Headquarters Staff and the tanks of A, B, and C Companies moved to Isigny where they were attached to the newly arrived 30th Infantry Division (Old Hickory).

In the waning days of June the 743d practiced coordinating combat maneuvers with infantry to improve the effectiveness of both. The disjuncture between infantry and tankers had been felt on the beach. In the days following, weak combat coordination had occasionally resurfaced, and at times lives were almost lost. On June 7, for example, Charlie Company's DD tanks were fired upon by infantry who mistook the unfamiliar shapes for enemy armor.[86] Shortly after sorting out the differences, the whole group came under friendly artillery fire.

In another incident, four days later, A Company tanks and a squad of infantry successfully assaulted and then bivouacked outside the small village of La Comte.[87] The tankers used their dozer blades to scoop out wide shallow trenches over which the tanks parked. Access to the earthen dugout was obtained from behind the tank and through the escape hatch located underneath the assistant driver's seat. In this way the crew safely relaxed, protected by the tank overhead, by the tracks along the sides, and in front, by the soil berm pushed up by the blade. One man from each crew stood watch in the turret with a Thompson machine gun and grenades close at hand.

Early the next morning, at 4 A.M., rustling noises in the surrounding underbrush brought the challenge of, "Halt! Who goes there?" The heavily accented "Me" brought a hail of gunfire from the turret. Roused to find themselves under enemy fire, crewmen shoved out from underneath the back of the tank or shinnied through the floor-mounted escape hatch. After fighting off the attack it was discovered that the infantry had withdrawn from the forward position without notice.[88]

An encounter on Omaha with poisonous gas had not been discounted by military planners.[89] In the face of this threat, tankers carried gas masks and wore specially treated clothing designed to prevent the passage of gas through to the skin. When the risk of chemical warfare faded, the rubber masks were stowed in compartments under the turret floor, and the coveralls were washed in gasoline to dissolve their special coating. One example demonstrates the seriousness with which the threat of gas was taken.

A Company's 3d Platoon tanks pulled under trees and beside ruined buildings. One by one the tank engines shut down and while some crewmen remained in the tanks and counted rounds, others dismounted and set about gathering fuel cans for a run back to the nearby beach and the supply depots being established there.

George Johnson moved slowly, his movements around the tank checked not only by the heavy tanker's coveralls, but also by an intense fatigue, the product of a long day strapped in a short-backed driver's seat. The battalion had had too little rest and far too little sleep since D-Day. The distant cry of "Gas!" sent crews scrambling and brought forth an energy that overrode the numbing lethargy. Johnson dropped into the turret and quickly passed up the masks stored there.

The snug-fitting masks altered the voice as if talking into tin cans. The excited tanker dashing from group to group searched in vain for an extra mask. Possessed by a wild-eyed look, the lonely figure nervously rushed about all the while yelling, "I'm a goner! I'm a goner!" The gathering crowd posed questions.

"What does it smell like?" one asked.

"I can't smell anything! I'm a goner!" the tanker cried.

"Do you smell anything yet?" asked another in his tin can voice.

"I can't smell anything!" the frightened man screamed.

The attention fixed on the forlorn tanker was interrupted by the appearance of a rattling, wood-sided truck, the slatted back stacked high with fuel cans. The cry of "Gas!" passed down the line of parked tanks was to alert the crews that the battalion's Service Company fuel trucks had just arrived from the beach.[90]

With the exception of a single Mark IV knocked out in the second day of fighting, the 743d exercised their superiority in armor and firepower against armored cars, artillery positions, machine gun nests and pill boxes. Off-road travel had proved rougher going, not only because of the difficult hedgerow-filled countryside, but also because of the defenders' ability to employ the terrain to their advantage. The beach assault was a bloody, difficult prelude to eleven months of almost continuous combat. On the beach the metamorphosis from theory to practice, civilians to soldiers had occurred, but it did not prepare the crews or their tanks for what was coming next.

II

The Sherman Medium Tank:
On the Front and in the Papers

WHOEVER WAS RESPONSIBLE FOR SUPPLYING THE ARMY WITH TANKS IS
GUILTY OF SUPPLYING MATERIAL INFERIOR TO ITS ENEMY COUNTERPART FOR
AT LEAST TWO YEARS OR MORE. HOW ANYONE CAN ESCAPE PUNISHMENT
FOR NEGLECTING SUCH A VITAL WEAPON OF WAR IS BEYOND ME.
> Hanson W. Baldwin, *New York Times*, Monday, March 19, 1945

WE'VE GOT THE FINEST TANKS IN THE WORLD. WE JUST LOVE TO SEE THE
GERMAN ROYAL TIGER COME UP ON THE FIELD.
> *Lieutenant General George S. Patton, Jr., replying to an article unfavorably comparing*
> *American and German tanks. Time, February 12, 1945*

BY the time the Allies re-entered northern Europe via the Norman
beaches, almost six years had passed since the German introduction
of the armored *blitzkrieg*. During this interim German armor had
been constantly improved.

America's experience against German armor in North Africa
had already demonstrated the inferiority of the Grants and early
model Sherman tanks. However, the African campaign had also
suggested the viability of using artillery and tank destroyers against
enemy armor. On December 1, 1941, under the recommendation
of Lieutenant General Lesley J. McNair, the Tank Destroyer Center
at Fort Meade, Maryland was established to train tank destroyer
units.[1] Tank destroyer units were America's answer to the German
armored *blitzkrieg* that had contributed greatly to the allied disaster

at Dunkerque the previous year. McNair envisioned tank destroyer units engaging and destroying enemy tanks to provide breakthroughs for armored divisions. The Sherman medium tank, and its earlier counterpart, the Grant, were to be the flexible, mobile appendage of the tank destroyer concept. The General Sherman was designed to spearhead and exploit breakthroughs into an enemy's rear area. It was not designed for static tank battles. However, as the experiences of the 743d adequately demonstrate, breakthroughs most often resulted from the coordinated action of tank battalions and infantry, sometimes at a terrific cost to both.

The mission of American tank battalions during World War II was infantry support. Therefore, besides the three medium tank companies (A—Able, B—Baker, and C—Charlie) and one light tank company (D—Dog), each with its own mess and maintenance sections, tank battalions also contained a mortar and an assault gun platoon.

Armed with a 37 mm main gun and thinly armored, D Company's light tanks were extremely vulnerable. The 743d ultimately relegated its light tanks to reconnaissance and those missions where infantry support would not put the tankers into situations where they would be battling heavier German tanks. On the other extreme, the Assault Gun Platoon was made up of five Sherman tank chassis outfitted with a 105 mm main gun and known as M7s. Although the battalion's M7s served as armor, particularly in the Ardennes, the assault guns usually worked in conjunction with field artillery to soften up objectives at the outset of an operation. This platoon also operated independently with battalion forward observers and the 743d's mortar platoon to locate, disrupt or destroy enemy troop or armor concentrations.

The 743d's Sherman M4 series medium tank was developed in 1941 at Aberdeen Proving Grounds, Maryland, from the T-6 test vehicle that was in turn based on an earlier production medium tank model, the M3 Grant.[2] Mid-production M4s had a glacis or frontal hull thickness of 2.0 inches set at an angle of 56 degrees, whereas the sides of the hull were 1.5 inch-thick steel. The turret presented 3.0 inches of steel in the front with 2.0 inches at the sides. The battalion's M7 Assault tanks had about 1/2 inch more armor on the fronts of both the turret and hull, as did the later Sherman models M4A1, M4A2 and M4A3.[3]

Five men manned each tank. The tank commander sat or stood in the turret behind the gunner and loader or cannoneer who operated a .30 caliber machine gun. Below, on either side of the transmission and in front of the turret basket, sat the driver, and to his right the assistant driver (a position familiarly termed the bog seat), who also operated a .30 caliber machine gun mounted in the right front armor plate. Periscopes mounted in the hatches substituted for direct sight when the covers were closed.

Americans found the 32-ton Sherman, with an overall width of only 105 inches, well suited to narrow and often ancient European streets, roadways and bridges. The Sherman's simple maintenance, high mechanical reliability and rapid shooting, aided by its power traverse, quickly made it a popular tank among armored divisions. These same qualities endeared it to battalion tankers. As later recalled by Frank Lancaster of Charlie Company, crews seldom had to do more than check the oil, clean the air filter, and keep the fuel tanks full.[4]

One of the more peculiar models of Sherman tank was the amphibious Duplex-Drive (DD) tank used on June 6. The DD tank resulted from Americans' successful hybridizing of a flotation device first employed by British Valentine tanks in 1943. The basic unit consisted of a rubberized canvas screen fixed to the top of the tank hull that held back the water like the sides of a boat. Compressed air erected the screen by inflating 36 vertically-placed bladders attached to a similar number of metal struts. The canvas screen blocked the main gun when elevated and the bow machine gun when collapsed. Two propellers drove the tank when afloat.

After a January 1944 demonstration of the British invention, General Eisenhower ordered the secret flotation system for American use during the upcoming invasion. Within six weeks the first 100 American-built DD tanks arrived in Britain.[5]

Major William Duncan, later the commanding officer of the 743d, was appointed officer in charge of the American DD Tank training school located in southern England.[6] Colonel Duncan's school trained A, B and C Companies of the 743d, 741st, and 70th Tank Battalions. Invasion plans required that troop landing craft (LCMs) transport the new DD tanks to their launching areas off the Norman coast. Duncan's training school soon discovered that tank-filled LCMs, designed to transport men, overturned easily. During one training accident using LCMs three Able Company tanks and their crews perished. Another crew survived only because the tank lodged crossways on the deck. A second fatal accident in April of 1944 assured that the battalion would never launch its DD tanks in rough waters.

Prior to the invasion of Normandy the battalion tankers lived and trained at Torcross, a village above Slapton Sands on the south coast of England. Amphibious exercises were performed during the week with the support of British naval rescue craft from Dartmouth. These craft returned to their port for maintenance and servicing on weekends. It was at Torcross on what should have been a quiet April Sunday afternoon, that battalion tankers were approached by an officer just down from London desiring to see how a DD tank "floated" in. Because of the rough sea and the absence of naval support, Colonel Duncan declined to accommodate the officer's wish, asking instead that he return on a weekday when the sea, and more importantly, rescue conditions were better. The officer attempted to force the issue and persuaded a lieutenant to "volunteer" his tank and crew. Colonel Duncan watched the skirt of the tank go up and wade into the ocean; then he returned to his office overlooking the channel.

> When it was about fifty yards out and swimming I heard a shout and I ran to the window and saw it sinking. The breakers had been too strong and crushed the skirt. I hurried to the phone and called the British Naval Duty Officer at Dartmouth's Navy Yard and asked them to send a rescue craft immediately. I ran onto the beach and sent an officer to our supply room to get as much rope as he could and life jackets and life rings. I then called for volunteers from our strongest swimmers. Two men thought they could swim out to where the tank crew members were trying to swim in their life jackets. One man got to shore by himself. The strong current was rapidly carrying the men out to sea. One of the swimmers towing a rope reached one crew member and pulled him in. One of the other swimmers with the rope got to the lieutenant who refused help and told the rescuer to swim on to a crew member who was further out. Before the rescuer could get to the crew member farther out he developed cramps and we had to pull him in. So we still had the lieutenant and two men in the ocean.[7]

Battalion members ran along the beach waving back and forth trying to keep sight of the remaining crewmen as the tide pushed the men in their life preservers through the cold channel waters. After about twenty minutes the men stopped waving, then one disappeared from sight. When the British rescue boat arrived, two sailors jumped into the water and brought the lieutenant and one man aboard. Although both men were provided with emergency treatment en route to a Plymouth hospital, one man died while still onboard the craft, the other died at the hospital from exposure.[8]

The decision to bring the battalion's tanks into the beach on June 6 saved the lives of the medium tank crewmen and must surely be attributed to experiences with rough water landings at Torcross, including the accident of April 28.[9]

Tank battalions were on the low end of the armored totem pole, an unenviable position considering American armored tactics and vehicles changed little in the ten months following June 6, 1944. The shortcomings of a specialized tactical theory (dependent upon a weapon designed especially for rapid moving armored divisions) was sorely felt at the battalion level. The tank battalions attached to infantry divisions fought and moved at the foot soldiers' pace, battling over limited terrain against static, well-defended positions. However, this in itself was not the greater hardship. The significant difficulty was that the tanks supporting German infantry, although slower, were better armored with bigger guns and therefore suited to close-in, armored battle.

While shiploads of American Shermans were being unloaded in England, behind the scenes, an ongoing dispute was being waged between the Armored Force's preference for a heavier battle tank, based on expanding battlefield experience, and the Army Ground Forces' contention that tanks could be countered best by artillery and tank destroyer units. The inability of either side to overcome the objections of its opponent aggravated an increasingly difficult battlefield situation. The specialized Tank Destroyer unit theory, conceived after limited battlefield practice, hobbled American tank development so much that the Allied battle for western Europe would depend almost exclusively upon the Sherman M4 series tank through to the end of hostilities. Perhaps the only viable solution in the face of battlefield and industrial reality were the piecemeal improvements regularly made to the M4's hull, armaments, and chassis. But improvements could not come fast enough from engineers' drawing boards and army testing grounds to the battlefield.

Following the breakout from the Anzio beachhead, American reporters in Italy identified the deficiencies of American armor, but General Devers, the American theater commander in Italy, quickly suppressed all publicity.[10] In the end, military censorship had little real effect. At home, articles had already begun appearing such as "Tanks need thicker hulls if they are to survive" (1943), and "Smoke marks U.S. tanks" (1943).[11] As could be expected, the differences between Axis and Allied armor did not go unnoticed in northwestern France where, in the wake of further negative press coverage of the Sherman's defaults, General Montgomery followed Dever's lead.

Difficulties with the General Sherman were first publicized by front-line reporters working in northwestern France for CBS under Edward Murrow's direction.[12] Douglas Edwards, in his broadcast of June 17, 1944, noted the great numbers of tank losses in the Norman campaign, a subject he returned to in his report of July 20.[13] William

Henry began his July 31 report announcing the possibility of a congressional investigation into the quality of American tanks.[14] American reports encapsulated the numerous difficulties encountered by nearly all Allied tankers fighting the Normandy campaign.[15]

In July 1944, while the battle for Normandy was under way, General Eisenhower initiated an investigation of tank problems and ordered Brigadier General Joseph A. Holly, Chief of the Armor Section for the European Theater of Operations, to speed up procurement of better armed tanks.[16] However, the industrial interval needed to develop the necessary production facilities for the new model Sherman tank convinced American commanders to await the delivery of the new 90 mm Pershing.[17]

As could be expected, journalistic interest in the tank problem was intimately related to the waxing and waning of major battles. Hence, at the end of August 1944, after the bitter encounters of the Falaise Gap, when large scale armored conflicts in western France dropped, there was a corresponding drop in the attention given the tankers' dilemma. Only Von Rundstedt's December offensive in the Ardennes refocused journalists' attention on the issue of tanks.

The difficulties with American armor in Normandy, and later the Ardennes, and the need for improvements had not gone unnoticed in Washington D.C. Although unable to supply 90 mm Shermans, the government tried to reassure the public that it was in control and not overwhelmed by the too-little-too-late theory expounded by the press. Roosevelt included a reference to the tank issue in the twelfth State of the Union Address, delivered January 6, 1945.

> . . . we cannot afford to fight the war of today or to-morrow with the weapons of yesterday. For example, the American Army has now developed a new tank with a gun more powerful than any yet mounted on a fast moving vehicle. The Army will need many thousands of these new tanks in 1945.[18]

Hanson Baldwin exemplified journalists' efforts to serve as the tanker's voice at home. Baldwin knowledgeably discussed the tank problem in a three-part article published mid-March 1945 in the New York Times, citing facts that would be publicly denied by the government, as the struggle with tank improvements continued behind the scenes.[19] This was not Baldwin's first foray into the question of tank procurement. In the concluding installment of an earlier series of reports concerning Von Rundstedt's Ardennes offensive, Baldwin had highlighted the Sherman's inferiority against the German tanks.[20] It was these earlier criticisms that Baldwin elaborated upon in his March articles.

Baldwin was not alone. *Newsweek* war correspondents Henry Paynter and Roland C. Gask had filed an article for the February 26, 1945 issue of their magazine citing the same problems examined by Baldwin.[21] Other reports emphasizing the inferior nature of American armor also appeared. In a *Newsweek* article entitled "Decision to the Tiger," it was recalled that the magazine had published a photo in 1943 showing an early model Tiger tank in Tunis, North Africa. Although at that time *Newsweek* had suggested that the Tiger's main gun was an 88 mm, the Ordnance Department in Washington D.C. replied that the reporters' identification was erroneous, and that in fact, it would be impossible to mount such a large gun in a tank turret.[22] Tanker complaints were bravely aired also in an issue of the *Stars and Stripes*, an unlikely place to find public discussion of such topics.[23]

The journalistic call for new or improved tanks culminated with a three-page illustrated article in the March 26, 1945, issue of *Life*.[24] *Life* illustrators compared the Sherman, Stalin, and Tiger tanks according to thickness of armor, tread width, armor piercing capability, incline climbing and fording ability. Unlike the more restricted or regional distribution of the *New York Times* or perhaps *Newsweek*, *Life* cut through the strata of American society, graphically revealing the Sherman's shortcomings to the general public. The *Life* article was the journalists' last entry in their call for a new tank.

Hanson Baldwin's articles were by far the more detailed discussions of the period. Some of the tankers' complaints summarized by Baldwin were:

1) the Sherman had a too high profile;

2) when struck during battle the gas powered engine often ignited, enflaming the whole tank;

3) the frontal armor plate was too thin;

4) a more powerful main gun was needed, with muzzle brakes to reduce the amount of blowback during firing that could temporarily blind the tank crew;

5) the tracks were too narrow;

6) tank compasses were inoperable.

Still, no amount of rhetoric, neither political nor journalistic, could change rapidly enough the shortcomings of a political, industrial and military reality.

When examined fifty years later, many tank problems can be seen as reflecting the confused nature of tank development in relation to McNair's perceived role for the Sherman tank and the use to which it was being put. Moreover, despite the public's impression, it was known prior to June 1944 that heavier tank guns were needed. In the spring of 1944 tanks outfitted with a more powerful 76 mm gun were hurried to Britain's Imber Firing Range for demonstration, but there was a reluctance, among American commanders, to change guns on the eve of battle.[25] And besides, a more powerful gun was contrary to the proposed purpose of the tank. After witnessing the Imber demonstrations, then-Lieutenant General Patton indicated he would only accept the heavier gun *after* combat testing in tank battalions.[26]

For the reader a simple exercise can be made using this page. Imagine the page to be a field. Now divide the page vertically into thirds. Each third will represent 400 yards, with, say, a German Mark V Panther tank with its standard 88 mm gun at the top and a 75 mm Sherman M4 at the bottom. The reader must then imagine the following scenario: as the Sherman enters the field, its tank commander identifies his target and proceeds to travel two-thirds of the distance up the page to achieve an effective disabling shot. Open terrain put the Sherman and its crew into immediate danger. The tank commander maneuvers as he advances, seeking to take advantage of whatever cover from fences to trees and bushes the Sherman can benefit from. In our scenario we will assume that the Sherman closes unobserved to within 500 yards, that is within the last two thirds of the page. Two shots are possible, one to the turret race to prevent the Panther from using its slower power traverse to bring direct fire onto the Sherman, or a shot to the Panther's tracks to disable and perhaps force the abandonment of the heavier tank.[27] In either case the Sherman's commander will try to maneuver even closer for a final shot into the Panther's thinner side armor. In this scenario, as in actual combat, the burden of offensive warfare is clearly on the crew of the Sherman. In fact, if the tank had been observed and remained exposed for a long enough time, the Panther could have disabled or even destroyed the Sherman before it had left the bottom of the page. Tests in August 1944 at Isigny, France, barely two months after the Norman invasion, demonstrated that it was impossible to penetrate the frontal armor of the German Panther tank at over 300 yards with a 76 mm gun.[28]

Not even the thicker corner armor of the Sherman's turret offered adequate resistance to heavy caliber German antitank weapons. When an infantry commander assured 1st Lieutenant John Shanafelt that the road ahead was firmly in the hands of his troops, he moved his tank deeper into the front line and at first encountered only machine gun nests.

I was tracking these guys with my turret mounted 50 caliber. I had traversed the turret to exactly 90 degrees to the road we were sitting on so that when the German anti-personnel (AP) shell hit us it hit right up on the front corner of the turret. So it wasn't just going through six inches it was going through 10 inches of armor plate but it still came through and took off half the loader's head.[29]

The first shot knocked out the radio and now a second round ricocheted off the gun mantlet, splattering Shanafelt with shrapnel. Shanafelt grabbed a length of radio antenna and guided his tank out of line from the top of the turret by poking it through the open driver's hatch. Out of further danger, Shanafelt sought out the battalion's medics.

Some days later I was digging in my musette bag for something and I found a piece of shrapnel the size of my fist buried inside. That bag had been sitting right behind me on the radio. I have no idea how close that piece came to taking off my head too.

In the case of muzzle brakes, as with other minor modifications, it is difficult to ascertain why they were not immediately available since they had already been developed and tested on 76 mm guns in 1943.[30] Problems with compasses would never be resolved prior to the end of hostilities. 743d tankers carried hand-held prismatic compasses, usable only outside the all-steel tank.[31] The dangers posed by gas-powered engines which could and often did ignite, claiming many lives, is far less problematic.[32]

European theater American forces used Sherman tanks powered by gasoline stored in two reservoirs flanking the top of the sloping rear engine deck. To forestall the spread of a fire the driver, or someone standing beside the rear deck, could activate two carbon dioxide extinguishers connected to six nozzles surrounding the engine compartment. Two portable extinguishers were available also; one was located beside the driver, the other beside the loader in the turret basket. But these precautions had little effect. If an enemy round penetrated the engine compartment and ignited the 175 gallons of 80 octane fuel, it was almost certain that in the resulting inferno, the tank's 97 rounds of 75 mm would burn off as well as other ammo. Fires spread rapidly throughout the hull, fed by the highly flammable interior wall paint and the layer of lubricants spilled on compartment floors.[33] Diesel-powered engines would have reduced the tremendous risks involved with gas flameups. However, in March of 1942 the War Department ordered that only gas-powered vehicles would be used by U.S. forces overseas.[34] Consequently, the M4A2 diesel-powered Sherman was retained for stateside training or supplied to Great Britain, the Soviet Union and Free French Forces in North Africa.[35]

To enhance crew safety, factories welded inch-thick applique armor plates over the sponson ammunition racks, one on the left and two on the right. Tankers on the front line applied layers of steel, sand bags, or cement over the fronts of their tanks where the glacis, barely 2 inches thick, offered little real protection and few chances of crew survivability. Although these measures provided additional crew protection, the extra weight quickly fatigued suspensions and tracks. During battle the first rounds tearing through the bags weakened the protective layer, and frequent rebagging was necessary whenever the opportunity arose.

In spite of the field improvements, close-in combat remained unpredictable against even low caliber German antitank guns, as demonstrated by an incident recounted by Corporal Harlan Whitcomb.

The tank commander directed us around a corner and we started up a street spraying machine gun fire in the upper windows of the building to our left. Suddenly, we were hit with a loud bang and a shell was spinning around on the bottom of the turret. We had got hit by a 57 mm antitank shell killing our gunner. We backed out of range and I had to help pull the gunner out and lay him on the back of the tank. I was also wounded below the left knee. Up to this point I was a PFC, when I was moved over to the gunner's position I was automatically made a Corporal.[36]

Remarkably enough, the disparity between American and German tanks was a recent development. Prohibited by the 1919 Treaty of Versailles from building tanks, the German military restarted tank production in 1933, and by 1939 they had produced nearly 2,700 tanks, approximately half of which were the Mark I and II models. The former carried only machine guns whereas the latter sported a 20 mm gun. The 16-ton Mark III carried a 37 mm gun and weighed twice as much as the Mark II. With its 1.3 inch-thick frontal armor, this tank was comparable to the light tanks of the 743d. In 1939 the heaviest German tank was the 19-ton Mark IV with, at that time, 1.5 inches of frontal armor and a 75 mm main gun.[37] The real contribution of these thinly armored vehicles was their mobility.

In 1940, the Allied armies enjoyed a slight advantage in tank numbers.[38] Allied superiority in tank numbers and quality continued into 1941 despite the introduction of the German Mark IV with its 75 mm gun. The Mark IV was the heaviest German tank of the time and primarily reserved for infantry support. Although the Germans later upgraded the Mark III, its low velocity 50 mm gun did not surpass the British Matilda's 2-pounder, and the Valentine, Crusader, and Stuart all provided better armor.[39] It was only in late 1941, early 1942, two years prior to the Normandy invasion, that the Germans began a series of models and model improvements that established a clear technological lead. The armor of the Mark III and Mark IV was doubled as a result of battlefield experience in Russia. But with the introduction of the American Grant in May 1942, the German High Command believed the Allies were again tending towards a superior position with respect to armor.[40] Certainly, German doubts about their tank quality were dispelled at Kasserine Pass in February 1943 after encountering the American Second Corps under General Dwight D. Eisenhower.[41] In July of the same year, 300 miles south of Moscow in the fields of Kursk, the Germans introduced tanks outfitted with 88 mm antiaircraft guns. These were the medium weight Mark V Panther with 4 inches of frontal armor and 1.8 inches of side armor, and the Mark VI, Henschel Tiger which also had 4 inches of frontal armor but with 3.2 inches on the sides. The additional frontal armor made these tanks impregnable against the American 75 mm and 76 mm guns. They would be the bane of the American medium tank for the remainder of the war.

A heavy battle tank existed in American arsenals. The M6 tank weighing 60 tons—almost twice that of the M4—and carrying a 3-inch antiaircraft gun in its turret was a production tank in 1940.[42] Because of transport problems and uncertainties about its performance on European streets and bridges the M6 never saw combat in Europe. In addition, a joint project involving representatives of the Chief of Ordnance, Aberdeen Proving Grounds, and the British Tank Mission developed the T-14, between 1942 and April 1943, as an intermediary between the American heavy and medium tanks.[43] T-14s weighed approximately 47 tons (15 tons more than the Sherman), and had a maximum speed of 24 mph, but it still bore the Sherman's 75 mm gun. Pilot T-14s were being constructed in 1943 when the project was scrapped.[44] The decision to drop this tank model was not due solely to technical problems. The American army had no real interest in a heavier battle tank. Tacticians maintained that tank destroying was for artillery and tank destroyers. Thus, early in the fall of 1943 (the same time as the formal rebuff of *Newsweek*'s identification of the Tiger's 88 mm), Army Ground Forces rejected mounting a 90 mm antiaircraft gun on the Sherman because of concerns that such powerful guns would encourage tank battles, a role outside that defined for a weapon of exploitation.[45] This decision discarded the industrial preparation time Brigadier General Holly required the following year when pressed by General Eisenhower to provide 90 mm Shermans.[46]

In early 1945 the War Department's answer to press, soldiers, and families was to reassure them that the new Pershing, T-26, with its 90 mm main gun, announced by President Roosevelt's State of the Union Address, would soon be available.[47] After a four-week European battlefield tour, Major General Levin H. Campbell, Jr., Chief of Ordnance, was quoted in *Time* magazine as defending the American High Command's preference for "lighter, nimbler armor."[48] In the same article, another quote attributed to General Eisenhower stating, "We have knocked out twice as many tanks as we have lost," caused *Newsweek*'s Wes Gallagher to respond that this figure represented German vehicles destroyed by all weapons, not those destroyed by tanks alone.[49] Only continued devastating battlefield experience would suffice to convince key decision makers that tank design was improperly perceived, and that battles between American and German tanks were inevitable.

Battlefield experience was not lost on the men of the 743d. Sergeant Alvin Tisland decided he would get a Tiger tank for his own, promising his C Company commander he could go all the way to Berlin with a tank of such quality. The opportunity arose during the Siegfried Line Campaign when a lucky shot from Tisland's gunner decapitated a Tiger tank commander. Minutes later, the remainder of the crew abandoned the unharmed and unmoving Tiger. Tisland recognized his chance and obtained permission to not only retrieve the tank, but also to repaint it and use it.

Tisland hefted the commander's body out of the turret, and settled into the driver's seat, grinning as the ignition brought the tank to life. The engine purred and the great tank rolled forward a short distance, then jerkily stopped. Nothing he tried revived the engine. Tisland abandoned the project, despairing of achieving his goal.[50]

The 743d's engagements with enemy tanks remained light until the tough, decisive July battles in the hedgerowed countryside surrounding Saint-Jean-de-Daye. The Norman hedgerows became the proving ground for innovations in battalion-level tank tactics. The 743d's invaluable experiences, gained at enormous cost in the Norman fields, determined the unit's successes in the then unimaginable tank battles in the extreme cold, snow, and darkness of the Ardennes and the Ruhr valley. Continued combat in the Sherman M4 would prove that survivability was a mixture of battle-acquired skill coupled with eleventh-hour field improvements and the unexplained which can only be ascribed to luck.

III

Seven for Eleven

WE WERE BASTARDS. WE WOULD FIGHT ALONGSIDE WHOEVER NEEDED US. AND WE WERE BASTARDS IN RANK. WE KNEW RANK, SO YOU DIDN'T HAVE TO WEAR IT, AND WE HAD RESPECT, A LOT OF RESPECT.[1]

Sergeant Perry "Cock" Kelly, A Company

THE ATTACHMENT OF A TANK BATTALION TO AN INFANTRY DIVISION WAS A SORT OF TENUOUS ARRANGEMENT AS FAR AS COMMAND WAS CONCERNED. IT WOULD MEAN THAT FOUR TANK COMPANIES WOULD WORK WITH THREE INFANTRY REGIMENTS. THIS WOULD SPREAD [FOUR COMPANIES OF] THREE PLATOONS, OF FIVE TANKS EACH, TO ASSIST THREE REGIMENTS. THE THREE INFANTRY REGIMENTS WOULD HAVE THREE BATTALIONS EACH, AND EACH INFANTRY BATTALION WOULD HAVE THREE COMPANIES. THIS LEFT COLONEL DUNCAN WITH A STRUGGLE TO SEE THAT WE WERE NOT OVER COMMITTED.[2]

Captain Joel Matteson, A Company

JULY: GREEN DEATH[3]

Freed from the restrictive coastal operations of June, battalion tanks moved farther inland, down country lanes and across fields. Spaced twenty to thirty yards apart, groaning machines would momentarily disappear in golden clouds of dust tainted by the acrid smell of burnt high octane fuel. In the ubiquitous Norman apple orchards, the high profile turrets snapped off smaller branches and caused unripened apples to drop like green stones into open turrets.

— 37 —

Characteristic of the 743d's time in combat was the ever changing context in which battle was experienced. Nonetheless, parts of hard learned lessons were always applicable elsewhere in some form or another and so it was with the battles for the hedgerows between the Vire River and Mortain.

War had not been a frequent visitor to Normandy. The most recent conflict had pitted French against French in the merciless contests between revolutionists and monarchists. The scars of that time were manifested in the inherited political sentiments which then, as today, ran stronger in the cities than in the countryside. In contrast, the scars of 1944 not only mark the men, women and children of that time but also the earth, from which reminders of war's passage are still recovered today.

The Norman countryside nurtures a perennial continuity derived from the natural rhythms and artificial alliances between man, his crops and his animals. Generations of Norman farmers had divided and subdivided the rich farmland into a patchwork-like quilt of fields known to the French as the *bocage*. This characteristic trait of the Norman topography became popularly known abroad by the English word hedgerow. Of the two terms, *bocage* is the more accurate since in one word a reference is made not only to the trees and undergrowth surrounding the field but also to the levees on which they are planted and the area they enclose. The battles of July and August 1944 were shaped, focused and measured by the *bocage*, the hedgerow terrain. It is necessary to know the region in order to appreciate and understand the battlefield tactics of that time.

The Norman *bocage* harbors renewable, seasonal bounties such as firewood, berries, small animals and the game birds crucial to subsistence-level family farms. This natural richness complements the cultivation of oats, vegetables, and various kinds of orchards. Natural borders of seemingly unmanaged growths of oak and bramble surround fields that are sometimes only yards wide. At intervals in the luxuriant entanglement, better known to owners than to haphazard visitors, are passages wide enough for a cart or plough and a team of draft animals. Not all the fields are open, planted terrain, nor are they all flat. Many are mere garden patches on the rolling countryside.

The *bocage* is an area-wide phenomenon. Prior to the invasion, the 743d and other units knew that they would be fighting in countryside chopped up into postage stamp-size parcels and had even practiced among similar fields in England. On the continent the line companies, Assault Gun Platoon and Headquarters Company continued practicing with their attached infantry on how best to approach or bypass the overgrown barriers.[4] The Norman fields became the testing ground for new techniques in infantry and tank cooperation and survival in its grander sense.

Ever ready to take advantage of whatever defensive opportunities local terrain offered, the Germans made the mosaic-like fields into a deadly maze peppered with antipersonnel mines, antitank mines, camouflaged tanks, snipers, machine guns and infantry toting antitank weapons. Machine guns outfitted with cords were placed in difficult to defend locations. A tug on the cord concentrated the attackers' attention on the machine gun fire and away from the actual location of the defenders who would harass the attackers from their flank or rear. Heavier machine guns were located at either end of the larger fields, sheltered in the deep drainage ditches dug along field perimeters. Strategically sited riflemen supported the machine gun crews. Some of these soldiers acted as tree-located snipers; others were equipped with the lethal shoulder-fired, armor-piercing *Panzerfaust*. The battalion and infantry soon discovered that the surest means of survival demanded the quickest cross-field attack possible.[5]

In an early attempt to overcome the natural and manmade barriers Captain John McCoy, of the 743d, ordered steel rails salvaged from the Omaha beach obstacles cut into short lengths and welded, like stubby fingers, onto the tank fronts. When assaulting a hedgerow, the tank commander would select, then ram, the lowest berm, generally five feet or less in height. The tankers braced themselves against the shock of the impending impact. The force of a 32-ton tank striking the berm threw up soil, roots, leaves, and branches, temporarily blocking drivers' vision. In hedgerow busting the element of surprise was difficult to maintain and so to confuse its defenders, tankers were sometimes requested to bust up to ten holes into the same field.

The tactic that was more widely adopted by the 743d called for the detonation of dynamite charges set within the ancient massive root systems anchoring the hedges. The detonation coincided with the scream of a siren mounted on the tank leading the attack through the freshly blown breach. The next two tanks passing the opening broke to either side of the leader while raking the opposite tree line with machine gun fire. If all went well, the infantry swept in from behind, accompanied by the platoon's two remaining tanks. After crossing, the surviving combat elements of a force rallied at the opposite side of the field, took up new positions, and prepared for the next assault. A variation of this tactic called for simultaneously blowing three holes with three tanks attacking abreast through the three openings followed by the remaining tanks and attached infantry.

To facilitate the new berm-breaching technique, 743d tankers started carrying dynamite on the rear deck above the engine compartment. Although this was welcomed by the already over-burdened footsoldier it introduced a new terror to the world of the tanker.

Two hazards confronted tankers carrying large quantities of dynamite on their rear tank deck. First, was the German light artillery zeroed in on the fields and the 88s strategically located to give across-field direct fire. Secondly, even if the crew were fortunate enough to escape a direct hit, the explosion from an artillery round could ignite the dynamite. Fed by the dynamite, the fire would quickly spread downwards to the engine compartment, disabling the tank. In seconds the flames entered the turret where exploding fuel or ammo killed, maimed or stunned crews, rendering them unable to evacuate their hull.

One incident relates how Private Graves' tank was struck by an enemy shell that simultaneously set fire to the dynamite on the rear deck:

> Almost instantly the engine compartment at the back was in flames. These spread quickly to the turret. The clothes of the tank commander, gunner, and cannoneer caught fire. The driver, stunned by the force of the explosion when the shell struck the dynamite sat "frozen" to his controls. Graves, himself burning, pushed the driver by sheer force up through the driver's hatch and out on the ground. Crawling out of the driver's hatch himself, Graves noticed the predicament of the three stunned men in the turret. His own face blacked and burned, Graves leaned down into the flaming turret and helped the rest of the crew out. All this time artillery was bursting around the tank and the incessant snipers were trying to pick off the men.[6]

A tactic used by the Germans to great effect, and one that allowed German commanders to nurture their valuable armor for later use, was a major line of defense combining 88 mm antitank guns with antitank and antipersonnel mines. In order to bypass the mine-ridden fields, 30th Infantry Division (Old Hickory) troops mounted the tank's rear deck. When the attackers struck the antitank mines, camouflaged German guns often destroyed the disabled tank while snipers picked off the isolated infantry and surviving crewmen.[7]

If manmade obstacles were not enough then rain in the bocage could easily jeopardize a rapid cross-field advance. Heavy rainfall forced tanks to keep to the roads. George Johnson's experience one drizzly afternoon was not uncommon. Johnson was guiding his tank down a rain-moistened highway when he spotted mines scattered over the roadway. The tank struck out cross-country and quickly became mired in mud. Unable to move, two crewmen dismounted to eat and were wounded by enemy artillery. Johnson and his crew left the tank and went to seek the company's T-2 tank recovery vehicle. Upon returning, the crew discovered that infantry had carried off all the machine guns.[8] Offroad travel during bad weather remained a problem even when months later metal track extensions were provided for the Sherman M4's narrow 17-inch wide tracks. The extensions were expressly designed to provide better traction and keep vehicles from miring in muddy conditions.

On the battalion's 31st day of combat the 743d was still without a respite, still on the move, and preparing to cross the Vire-Taut Canal at Pont-de-Saint-Fromond in support of the 30th Division's 117th and 120th Infantry Regiments. Among the many new replacements accompanying the battalion was Ashley Camp, whose soft spoken southern accent was a rarity in a battalion dominated by the quick, clipped speech of Minnesotans. Ferried across the Channel on June 13, Camp was awaiting orders in a replacement depot behind Omaha beach when Colonel Duncan, returning from the assault on Caumont, selected him and others as battalion replacements.

Camp was more than familiar with the Sherman M4 having spent considerable time at Fort Knox training for an armored division and instructing others in the use of the medium tank. Now, beneath a night sky, the Louisiana native was driving a clanking Baker Company tank along dark, narrow, tree-lined roads to a preassigned forward-staging area near the bridge of Saint-Fromond.

While the battalion moved into position, one tank platoon set off driving around another part of the front. The battalion successfully reused this decoy maneuver through to the end of the war.[9] On July 7, at 4 A.M., the sharp blasts of division artillery signalled the end of the decoy noise and the beginning of a barrage that continued for three hours.[10] The battalion's Assault Gun Platoon joined in with its six M7 tanks.

Under cover of dark and the ear-splitting artillery barrage the battalion's light and medium tanks gathered in their forward assembly areas. In the distance, beyond the trees shielding the waiting tanks, the unseen horizon was lit by the irregular brilliance of exploding artillery. The tankers sat beneath their open hatches, listening through sweat-moistened leather headgear to last minute orders and the rumble and crash of the artillery punctuating the sounds of the idling tank engines.

The attackers were not the only ones with artillery support. German counterbattery fire kept the tanks at bay, slowing the placement of treadway bridges across the 50-foot wide canal. Aided in their accuracy by the skillful use of predetermined ranges, the early morning German counterbattery fire was only an introduction to the often unexpected intrusion of enemy mortar and artillery.[11]

By midmorning Division engineers removed a wreck from the ancient stone bridge connecting the villages of Saint-Fromond and Airel and began replacing a damaged span with simple steel bridging. The battalion remained immobile in the undergrowth and orchards until the early afternoon when Able Company tanks crossed the bridge.

With advance elements of the 30th leading, 743d tanks struck out from the bridge in a northwest direction back along the Vire Canal towards Saint-Jean-de-Daye. The holding action the Germans had waged from their side of the canal was being challenged as the men and tanks spread into the surrounding countryside and battled late into the evening.

Early the next morning B Company was held in reserve with 2d Battalion of the 117th Infantry, near Pont-du-Saint-Fromond while the rest of the 743d renewed its attack. The objective was to push past Saint-Jean-de-Daye on route D8 and take the high ground near Le Desert. However, at six that morning, just as the attack began, the 2d SS Panzer Division, *Das Reich*, counterattacked. Already under way, A Company engaged the enemy first, losing two tanks with two men killed. Charlie Company fared better and was able to take a small hill near La Perine by overrunning the German position with its AT gun, armored car and several machine gun nests, but at a loss of two men killed and seven wounded. Another C Company tank working with the battalion's Mortar Platoon, had 2 crewmen wounded and one killed.

By midafternoon the warm, brightly lit morning had given way to cooler temperatures as dark-bottomed storm clouds advanced over the front. The clouds drew themselves like a cloak over the landscape, and the hard drumming of rain drops sounded nature's prelude to the crash of direct fire as the 2d SS Panzer Division counterattacked C Company positions at La Perine. German infantry, supported by six Mark IVs and Vs, probed for a soft spot in the front line. At La Perine only two Charlie Company Shermans were operable, one, that of Staff Sergeant Richard McCracken was without a radio. Nonetheless, McCracken moved forward to meet the attacking German column. Here for once the bocage proved its neutrality.

To communicate with his crew McCracken took two lengths of antenna and proceeded to guide the driver through the fields by prodding him on the back for straight ahead, left shoulder for left turn and right shoulder for right turn. As the rain fell into the open turret, McCracken guided his tank to a narrow between-field passageway in clear view of the advancing enemy armored column. Although the German tanks were only 500 yards away, still too far for the Sherman's 75 mm to have much effect, McCracken was well within range of the enemy tanks. McCracken's driver was positioning the lone Sherman in the opening between the fields when German mortar and artillery fire shattered their solitude. The gunner sent off the first round as the assistant driver sprayed the attacking infantry with his .30 caliber machine gun. In response, the whole of the enemy column turned and opened up on the tank. McCracken's loader slammed rounds into the breach as fast as they could be targeted and fired. All the while, enemy tank rounds whooshed by in near misses, or tore into the damp masses of foliage to either side of the tank. To keep their attackers at bay, the gunner depressed the barrel of the 75, sending every third round of HE into the enemy troops. McCracken's crew held their position, discouraging the advance of the German column. After black oily smoke signaled that one Mark IV had caught fire, the Germans broke off the skirmish to probe elsewhere, perhaps unwilling to risk the loss of additional armor. McCracken made sure no further advances were attempted, then used the antenna to guide his driver back out of the hole and into the rain-soaked, battle-scarred field. Further contest was useless, in the space of a few minutes all 97 rounds in the ready racks had been fired.[12]

On July 9, the 2d SS Panzer Division renewed its attack, this time lashing out at the positions of the 743d southeast of Le Desert.[13] The battalion's line remained firm and by late afternoon they claimed another antitank gun and armored car before returning to bivouac near Saint-Jean-de-Daye.

During the attack of the 9th it was Baker Company's 1st and 2d Platoons deployed with the 2d Battalion, 120th Infantry, that absorbed the brunt of the furious assault by German tanks supported by infantry and antitank guns.

German armored attacks supported by 88 mm antiaircraft/ antitank guns were a lethal combination. German roadblocks were placed so that the big 88 sighted down the exterior of a curve, with support vehicles concealed from return fire on the opposite side. When the 2d SS Panzer Division's vanguard encountered a brief loss of momentum, one of their antitank guns was across from Ashley Camp and a platoon of B Company tanks beside a farmhouse above a road.

Camp listened as the platoon leader ordered the first tank to lead the breakout around the house and onto the road. The tank commander responded that, faced with the 88, if he took his tank beyond the house they would be killed. Reminded in turn that he could follow through or be courtmartialed, the tank had moved scarcely ten feet when it was hit. Fully loaded with fuel and ammo the tank flamed up, consuming the crew members.[14]

Confronted with an unevenly enforced stalemate the remaining tanks in Camp's platoon sought another means of advance. The tanks followed a side route down to the road and were approaching the curve secreting the big German gun, when they encountered troops from the 2d Battalion, 120th Infantry, pulling back. With the appearance of the tanks the troops renewed their attack on the roadblock. When a member of the first tank was killed by antitank fire, crews were rearranged to keep the tanks operating. Camp now moved into a lower hatch position, but before going much farther, the tank quit running, just as the remaining two tanks were hit by direct fire. Deprived of their armored support, and having lost their commanding and executive officer, the infantry were ordered to withdraw.[15] The two operable Baker Company tanks provided covering fire for the retreating infantrymen, then withdrew, abandoning the destroyed or disabled tanks.[16]

On July 8, the previous day, nearly 100 tanks of Combat Command B, 3d Armored Division, crossed the bridge at Pont-du-Saint-Fromond, disrupting the 30th's roadnet and cutting field telephone lines. On the 9th the commander of 3d Armor's Combat Command B was relieved when his disorganized tanks failed to spearhead an early morning attack for the 30th's 119th Infantry Regiment. The same morning further difficulties for the 3d Armored Division developed when Combat Command A, attacking in front of the 30th Division's lines, took a wrong turn and ended up in a twenty-minute fire fight with the division's antiaircraft (AA) guns. When combined with the punishment being delivered by the 2d SS Panzer Division's attack on B Company tanks and the 120th Infantry, a near panic was almost achieved among some forward elements of the 30th Division. The division level response can serve as an indication of the real or perceived threat: within moments up to 18 battalions of artillery were firing onto the approach routes of the 2d Panzer until the enemy halted.[17] The battle to retake lost ground raged all along the front until nearly midnight. That night *Das Reich* withdrew and *Panzer Lehr*, moving down from the Bayeux area, slipped into position and prepared to assume its predecessor's work.[18]

On the morning of the 10th the battle began afresh with attacks by the tanks of Combat Command B, now under new leadership, to Hill 91, dominating Hauts-Vents and the crossroads at Pont-Hebert. Daytime progress was successful but under cover of night the enemy passed through the lines of infantry and tanks. The next morning it was discovered that the 902d Panzer Grenadier Regiment and a battalion of tanks were at work in the rear areas of the 30th Division, while *Panzer Lehr*'s tanks were hitting the neighboring 9th Infantry Division. The vicious two-pronged attack was halted by Combat Command B and early morning air strikes by P-47s. The German objective had been a bold attempt to split open the American front and push through to Isigny and the Norman coast.[19]

Due to the rising numbers of casualties among line company officers Captain Ed Miller was transferred from the battalion's Service Company to the command of Able Company. The stockily built, soft spoken Miller, who had never been trained for armor, found himself in command of a company of battle-hardened tankers.

The July 10 German counteroffensive had placed Hill 91 at Hauts-Vents once again into German hands and enemy artillery spotters were using it to their advantage. Counterattacks to retake the heights were being stymied by the hedgerows blocking cross-country vision and the bits of forest dominated by thin, towering trees that provided little security from the eyes of German observers. Ed Miller's tanks were locked in place, their advance paralyzed by artillery tree bursts wrecking the accompanying infantry.[20]

Because of the enemy artillery the infantry refused to move, even after Miller took his tanks forward 600 yards. During this time, a German Mark IV had closed unobserved to within direct-fire range. The first round from the Mark IV tore through the forward compartment of Miller's lead tank. Faced with the need to make an urgent decision, Miller devised a solution contrary to the practice of armored warfare. Miller took 1st Platoon, left the infantry behind, and tried to advance further when a *Panzerfaust* team fired on the tank. Miller turned his platoon into the forested undergrowth and suddenly found themselves overrunning the enemy's artillery communications position. As the Germans abandoned the site, the tanks crushed the sophisticated looking equipment under their tracks. After calling up the rest of A Company, 1st Platoon tanks scattered the remaining enemy troops by spraying their hilltop trenches with machine gun fire. With Hill 91 secured, the infantry rejoined the tankers, much to the relief of Battalion Headquarters that had been anxiously monitoring the tactics of the moment invented by the former Service Company commander. Tank action without infantry—the eyes of a tanker—was contrary to all armor training.

On the morning of the 13th the German counterattack raged into its fifth day. The enemy tried to exploit their limited gains by expanding their use of heavy mortar, artillery, antitank, direct tank fire and the *Nebelwerfer* rockets called Screaming Meemies. This time, elements of 743d's Baker Company, holding Able Company's former positions at Hauts Vents, repulsed repeated enemy counterattacks aimed at retaking the hilltop.

In the early morning of July 13, while manning a road block below Hauts Vents, Ashley Camp and other crew members were sitting beside their B Company tank eating breakfast when they were caught unaware by the *Panzer Lehr* counterattack.

Camp was writing a letter home when the quiet was shattered by a mortar round exploding in the apple tree beside the group. The air shook for a second time when a violent burst killed one man outright, and severely wounded Camp and D-Day veteran Jerry Lattimer. Treated by battalion medics the men were evacuated by air to England. It would be six months before they rejoined B Company for the Battle of the Bulge.

In one July operation, Wendell Jones led the charge into a field through an opening of a berm still choked with the dust and smoke from a dynamite blast. Jones was standing exposed in the turret, directing the machine gun fire of his assistant driver when he suddenly slumped down onto the metal floor. A sniper's bullet had entered his left temple, exiting on the right. Jones ordered his tank out of line, appointed a replacement commander, and after receiving a shot of morphine he laid down beside a nearby road. After several hours some medics happened along the dusty lane, administered another shot of morphine, and departed. Some time later yet another group stopped and had a short talk with Jones after which a jeep arrived. Jones was placed on a stretcher over the hood of the jeep and taken to a field hospital. During the whole ordeal Jones had maintained complete consciousness while holding his nose to slow the bleeding from his mouth. The following day he was sent by plane to England, and after recovering, assigned to guard duty at a P.O.W. camp near the very beach where the 743d had landed in June.[21]

Triage[22] was the standard approach to combat medicine during World War II. Under the practice of triage battlefield casualties were sorted according to the seriousness of the injury. Those men least likely to survive or receive the necessary medical attention quick enough, such as Jones, were given pain medication and attended last. Roving medics or corpsmen from "collecting companies" stabilized less serious injuries, and then the individual was transferred to a "clearing company" hospital. Farther behind the front line were the evacuation hospitals.[23]

To protect radio secrecy, call signs changed daily according to a code list distributed each morning. Tank locations and the names of crew members were not to be mentioned on the radio unless in the codes precribed for that day. Such guidelines applied less stringently to between-crew communications, but when switching to battalion net all such chatter was to conform to the daily code. This didn't always happen. Sometimes, when responding too quickly in an emergency the battalion net would be left switched on. In such instances the sight of a target would be announced to all.

"John do you see it?"

"Tank 14 get off the air!"

"On your left dammit!"

"Tank 14 switch off!"

"John!" might be called again before the tank interphone was reopened and the worries and excitement of a firefight would once again be limited to the confines of a crew's steel box.

From the outset of the Normandy campaign, poor communications plagued tank crews and the infantrymen with which they worked. T. Sergeant Ronald Hyland devised the battalion's solution. Hyland placed phones attached to the tanks' radio phone wires in ammo boxes on the rears of tanks. Hyland also developed a system whereby the infantryman's Walky-Talky could be used by GIs to contact tankers without having to stand behind a tank under fire.[24]

Ever since D-Day+1 the battalion's Service Company had brought fuel and other supplies forward to the line companies, all the while suffering the same losses as other companies. But battle often had its unbelievable measure of luck. One afternoon an enemy AP or HE dud, fired at a Service Company truck, pierced the side of the vehicle and passed through nine gas cans without any casualties.[25]

The battalion's lines held, but the ferocity of the Germans' repeated counterattacks was taking a horrific toll. During one week, from the start of the Vire attack on July 7 to the 13th, 30th Division lost a total of 3,200 officers and men dead, wounded and missing. The punishment received by tankers was no better.

At first the 743d's high casualty rate was met by rearranging companies to accommodate the losses. However, officers and tank commanders exposed in the high profile turrets were being killed or wounded in such alarmingly high numbers that over time a major reorganization of the line companies became necessary at the end of every day. Even these stop-gap measures became less and less effective. By July 14 the 743d's After Action Reports noted "Reorganizing Company, difficult problem as all Platoon sgts. and leaders have become casualties. New crews have to be established and trained."[26] As the casualties mounted, wounded men regularly remained with their companies.[27] Battlefield promotions became a common means of facilitating the reorganization process by providing some continuity in leadership. New replacements were incorporated at the lowest levels possible.

The enormity of the task assigned the 743d in its support role for the 30th Division is easy to appreciate. The 30th Division consisted of approximately 16,000 men of which 9,000 were divided into three Infantry Regiments, with three Rifle Battalions of 500 men each, containing three Rifle Companies of 189 men each. The battalion tanks were being constantly shifted, supporting an attack here, repulsing a counterattack there, or leading reconnaissance into another area. No individual in one company had any idea what the tanks of another company were doing. Only the colonel's headquarters staff, scrambling to try to meet every request, could say at any one time where battalion tanks were operating.

On July 14, the sixth day of the Vire battle, when Charlie Company was ordered to advance on La Viquerie, two tanks were left behind because no crews were available to man them. Two days later, on July 16, out of the whole battalion only C Company could go on mission; the other companies were in maintenance, repair, reorganization and training.

It was also on July 16, when battalion strength was at its lowest, that the Germans launched three successive armored counterattacks in an attempt to break the line held by the 30th's 120th Infantry and 13 C Company tanks.[28] In the ensuing two-day battle 16 German tanks were knocked out, 8 of these by the battalion.

In the countryside where the battalion frantically tried to reorganize, the situation remained one of unpredictable danger. Perry "Cock" Kelly had started with Able Company's Mess Platoon in 1942, back when the outfit was first organized at Fort Lewis, Washington. When July casualties required a shuffling of men, Cock quickly volunteered for line duty.

When mail call included a sister's present of real coffee, Cock treated it as the treasure it was, but discovered nothing was stowed in his new tank in which to prepare it. Cock spied a nearby bombed out farmhouse and set off, trudging across the open field between tank and farmstead.

He discovered on arriving that the farm buildings were being temporarily inhabited by 30th Division GIs. After securing a discarded pot in which to boil coffee, Cock again set out, container in hand, retracing his earlier route across the field.

The first mortar round seemed to come out of nowhere, exploding somewhere between him and the farmhouse he had just departed. Cock tucked the pot against his chest and broke into a run propelled by fear, zigzagging, ducking, and turning as exploding mortar shells stalked their elusive target. Corrected for distance, each shell measured Cock's progress across the field. With each explosion that rained dirt and stones, the pot was hugged even tighter until he reached the safety of the trees protecting the tank.

The German mortar team had come up short, but not by much. The next morning, Cock noticed that his trousers kept snagging on the backs of his legs and discovered that the skin was barbed with numerous hook-shaped metal splinters.

On the morning of the 18th a break in the battle allowed the 743d to move to the rear for maintenance and a much needed rest. Despite the battalion's enormous losses in men and material since the Vire canal jump-off, only seven miles had been gained in eleven days of slugging it out in the tangled hedgerows. Faced with unbearable losses of men and material, sandbagging was first tried. Sandfilled bags and ammo boxes were attached to the front glacis or sides of the turret by any means possible. Later, custom-made brackets were welded onto the exterior to hold the lifesaving layer. Sandbagging saved many lives. Among 743d tankers it quickly became a standard field improvement.[29]

The following day the city of Saint-Lo fell to the 29th Infantry Division, the same division that had fought alongside the 743d on the beaches of Omaha. News of the Saint-Lo victory was joined by the call of "Scouts Out!" Whenever the "scouts" were out, peeps and halftracks would unexpectedly appear at battalion roadblocks, and someone would distribute bottles of a dozen different kinds of alcohol—the fruit of the "Scouts'" efforts.[30]

The Americans were in a position to break the remaining German line at Hebecrevon, outside Saint-Lo, following their July 19 victory. The attack was conceived in the standard McNair strategy of 1941. An aerial bombardment would precede the attack of the tank battalions and infantry. The armored divisions, in attendance farther behind the front, would exploit the breakthrough.

Rain postponed the attacks of the 20th and 21st. The rain-soaked break from combat stretched to five days of reorganization and resupply. The storms provided additional time for the sandbagging of the remaining tanks and temporarily ended the enemy's nightly reconnaissance overflights. Indications of clearing weather allowed the return of much needed air cover, and as one battalion veteran, Harlan Whitcomb recalled, "We were glad to see them . . . at first."[31]

On the morning of the 24th, now somewhat protected by sandbags from direct, frontal-enemy fire, the battalions' assault units gathered in their forward staging areas to await completion of the aerial bombardment. At noon on that day the explosion of bombs among the assembled troops and tanks replaced the drone of incoming U.S. fighters and bombers. Shaken and angered men rushed to the aid of victims. For the most part, the 743d escaped relatively unharmed. Battalion casualties were limited to those individuals caught outside their tanks. But a real fear with a sense of helplessness and anger in such situations became ingrained in battalion veterans, feelings that would be justified again and again before the war was over.

On the morning of the 25th the debacle of the previous day seemed unrepeatable. Joel Matteson stood beside his tanks awaiting the order to move out. Matteson was commanding a platoon of Dog Company light tanks and, like Camp and many others, was a recent replacement, having joined the battalion shortly after its D-Day successes. As the menacing sound of the planes approached, men waited anxiously for the preliminary bombing to pass when suddenly to the horror of everyone it was realized that the bomb patterns were creeping ever closer to the assembled troops and tanks. The realization of oncoming destruction was met by the simultaneous crash of exploding bombs disguising the whistling of those still falling. The explosions shaking the air violently rocked the tanks, clumsily lifting their 32 tons off the ground. Caught outside the protective hull of his tank Matteson and four other men were severely wounded. Nearby, men pushed into already full foxholes only to be buried under cascading rain-dampened earth. Others sought safety under tanks that with each earsplitting blast seemed to press ever closer on the men underneath.

On the 25th, unlike the previous day when the bombs had stopped falling, the order was to go ahead with the attack. Dazed by fear and stunned by concussion, men stirred themselves to action. Ears were ringing, sounds were confusing, dust from the bombardment hung in the air, and nostrils stung from the bitter smell of explosives. Bits and pieces of soldiers and equipment had been strewn everywhere. Where trees still stood, canteens held by arms without bodies swung from branches. Many more had suffocated, buried alive by the dirt thrown up by exploding bombs.

Two columns moved forward. Men afoot skirted the macabre; the tanks drove over the dead.[32] Behind the advancing tanks and infantry, battalion medics and corpsmen moved to recover the living and those less fortunate. Joel Matteson was evacuated to England and would not return until early fall.[33]

Disbelief was replaced by anger at an unscathed and well entrenched enemy. The attack progressed to Hebecrevon where enemy armor was immediately encountered. Unfortunately, the tankers' fury and determination was not matched by a tank capable of sustaining frontal assaults.

All through the *bocage* the battalion's thin-skinned light tanks, armed only with 37 mm main guns, operated alongside the medium tanks—most often with disastrous results. One incredible incident involved a light tank that had successfully attacked across an open field. When it reached the opposite embankment, a German infantryman suddenly stood up at twenty feet and fired his shoulder-mounted *Panzerfaust*. The hastily aimed round spent its force on the front drive wheel and did not penetrate the thinly armored hull. The crew's point blank response didn't miss.[34]

Combat in a light tank was not always so easy. On the day following the second bombardment of 743d tanks and 30th Division troops, the battalion's light tanks moved out with the vanguard of the attack force.[35] One D Company light tank encountered three German Mark V Panthers and quickly fired off two shots. The uneven match was witnessed over the battalion's communication net and on site.

The German slowly began to wheel the 88 mm gun in its turret around towards the source of the annoyance. The American gunner fired once more and his dispairing voice was heard over the radio: "Good God, I fired three rounds and they all bounced off."[36]

Elsewhere, the battalion's medium tanks faired little better. Two Mark IVs were added to Able Company's list of kills at a cost of three of the battalion's M4 tanks. The following day A Company added another tank kill to its list while reinforcing nearby infantry positions. The push on Hebecrevon took on an urgent tone when by the end of the day the objective still had not been secured. 743d Charlie Company tanks and Old Hickory infantry refused air support and finally succeeded in overrunning the crossroad town. This allowed the 2d Armored Division to spearhead the subsequent days' attacks southeast towards Tessy-sur-Vire.[37] The 743d was now 45 days and four miles southwest of the village of Caumont, taken during their first week of combat.

The hedgerow battles were not yet over. When direct fire hit two 3d Platoon A Company tanks, the platoon leader dismounted to make his own foot reconnaissance. George Johnson watched as his tank commander reemerged from the bushes, motioning frantically with his arms. It was unclear what he wanted until he pulled out his .45 and started firing at a hedgerow. Johnson fired a round of HE in the direction the commander was shooting and blasted away the camouflage disguising an 88 mm antitank gun. Two more rounds sent the gun crew scurrying for cover.[38]

A common source of casualties among 743d tankers resulted from the need, realized early on in combat, to dismount and scout ahead either alone or with the accompanying infantry. Not only was a better understanding of the terrain possible, but men afoot were not as likely to be seen or heard as noisy tanks. Still, as often happened, the tanks could be spotted and those afoot could become the prey. There was no middle ground. On the afternoon of July 29, while attacking south of Le-Mesnil-Opac, two tanks stopped for reconnaissance and were caught by artillery judged to be 150 mm or larger. Both crews suffered heavily with three men severely wounded and four listed as missing in action.

The next day, July 30, A and B Companies resumed action in the area surrounding Le-Mesnil-Opac against enemy armor and antitank guns supported by machine guns. The fighting raged all day. Although Baker Company eventually knocked out one Mark IV, six Able Company tanks were lost. It was in this action that the first 743d POW was taken. After Lieutenant Hale's tank exploded, he escaped the flames only to be captured by attacking German infantry. Hale was later hospitalized in Paris.[39]

The following morning, with A Company in reserve, the attack continued its push towards a hill, forming a major part of the 2d Panzer Division's primary line of defense near Troisgots. The 117th, 119th, and 120th Infantry Regiments, supported by 743d Charlie Company tankers, attempted two attacks. Although three times as much artillery as normal was fired in support of the attacks, the Germans effectively paralyzed the advance by mounting their own simultaneous counter-battery fire and counterattacks. The Panzer troops successfully disabled one tank and burned another with the loss of all the crew. Unable to bypass or confront the hill, other remedies were sought.

On July 31 assistant gunner Harlan Whitcomb witnessed the end of the Troisgots impasse while operating a tank dozer in the platoon of Captain Harry Hansen. Whitcomb's dozer pushed a large hole through a hedgerow bordering an apple orchard, allowing three of the platoon's five tanks to cross. The platoon leader's dozer tank took a direct path across the field; the other two tanks broke to the left and right. Shortly after emerging from the opening, the left tank was struck by direct tank fire and burned with no survivors.[40] After crossing the field the tankers discovered they still were out of range of the German tanks. Hansen dismounted and led two infantry bazooka men into the nearby village of Troisgots. There, under intense enemy artillery and small arms fire the group knocked out two Mark VI Tiger tanks, one of which had just been battling against Hansen's attack. Hansen remained in the town until he located and directed artillery fire on a 105 mm self-propelled weapon until it too was destroyed.[41]

July had been hard on the battalion and its members. But it hadn't been any easier on the Germans. In a three-page memorandum written to Hitler, Rommel indicated that since June 6 ninety-seven thousand men had been lost, roughly 2,000 to 3,000 casualties per day, but he had been given only 6,000 replacements. Furthermore, of the 225 tanks destroyed by mid-month, just before the losses of the Battle of Mortain, he had received only 17 replacements.[42]

Of the battalions' 54 light and medium tanks, 38 were lost in combat, of which 33 were replaced. Sixteen crewmen were killed, 98 wounded and an additional 19 tankers listed as missing in action; losses equivalent to 26 tank crews. August was not to prove any better.

AUGUST: THE BATTLE OF MORTAIN

WE WERE TOLD THERE WERE ONLY A FEW MACHINE GUN NESTS OPPOSITE OUR NEW POSITIONS. WE QUICKLY FOUND OUT THERE WERE ALSO A BUNCH OF 88S.

Howard Froberg, B Company

Tuesday, August 1, the battalion bivouacked northeast of Saint-Romphire, France, cleaning equipment and doing much neglected maintenance work. Showers were available, the first since before D-Day, and a film was shown in the nearby church of Saint-Samson Bon Fosse. On Friday, a USO show provided another welcome distraction, followed by an address to the battalion by General Hobbs, 30th Division Commander.

The Saint-Lo breakthrough was achieved at great cost among the hedgerows, but allowed First Army to pass westward into Brittany and Patton's Third Army to move eastward through the Avranches gap into the enemy's rear.[43]

Released on Saturday August 5 of its duties near Saint-Lo the 30th was reassigned to VII Corps. On Sunday, Old Hickory and the 743d moved out together for new positions 40 miles southwest of the town of Vire, near the crossroad hamlet of Mesnil Rainfray. Troops and tanks followed the meandering course of the Vire River, prepared to exchange positions with the 1st Division beside Mortain.

While en route, the first enemy aircraft sighted since before Saint-Lo attacked the rear of the column with rockets. After arriving at their destination, most of the 743d was pulled up to guard the right flank of Old Hickory; only Charlie Company was kept in the hills northwest of Mortain on the division's left flank.

The Vire River cuts through the forested, low granite heights where the town of Vire sits amid the remnants of massive walls built by the son of William the Conqueror. In 1944, one medieval gate tower dominated the town and the countryside for miles around. From this lookout German sentries could see to the southeast beyond Soudeval towards the wooded hills sheltering Mortain. In July of 1944, Vire's granite church, on its granite hill, set amid the memories of past struggles, was now in the midst of yet another.

The Saint-Lo breakthrough had made the German situation in Normandy critical. And, although the Avranches push was under way, the Allies were still in a very tenuous position dependent upon the exploitation and expansion of a narrow coastal strip of Norman France. In addition, even after two months on the continent the uncertain quality of intelligence could be strongly felt. Unknown to the men of the 743d General Von Rundstedt's army was going on the offensive in an attempt to split the Allied forces by attacking what Rundstedt perceived as the weakest point in the Allies' southern line—the 30th Infantry Division's new position in the rolling countryside beside Mortain. Codenamed LUTTICH, 4 Panzer Divisions and their attachments prepared a counterattack destined for Avranches six miles away on the Norman coast.[44] On the evening of the 6th, while 30th Division troops and 743d tanks moved into place, German forces secretly assembled in an area immediately east of Mortain to await midnight.

The odds were against the Americans from the outset although the 30th was moving into positions occupying the high ground over a seven-mile front dominating the Sée River. Several factors would contribute to the initial successes of the German outbreak:

a. there was little knowledge of the German positions opposite the front lines of the 30th;

b. the battle started before the 30th was in place and before reconnaissance could begin;

c. the 30th was occupying positions unprepared for defensive action;

d. only seven Old Hickory battalions were available to defend the new seven-mile front. July battles had taken its toll. The division was still lacking 1,000 men.

Shortly after midnight the front erupted under a vicious barrage of artillery, mortar, and *Nebelwerfer* rockets.[45] The ferocious bombardment became the measurement with which battalion veterans compared all subsequent shellings. Three hours later the Germans struck from the north and south with a pincer movement on the roads leading into Mortain, squeezing out the Americans caught in between.

As the cool dawn developed into full light, the German attack benefited from the fog rising from the Sée River. All that could be determined was that German tanks and infantry, principally from the 2d Panzer Division, were present throughout the American positions in some areas to a depth of 6 miles. American infantry suffered as much from German-inflicted casualties as from disorganization and battlefield isolation.

A second German blow was thrown at the center of the 30th located at Saint-Barthelemy. Under cover of darkness and fog 50 tanks of the 1st SS Panzer Division supported by the 2d SS Grenadier Regiment pounded at and then overran the 1st Battalion 117th Infantry Regiment. Saint-Barthelemy would remain a hot spot for the next five days.

On the afternoon of the first day of the Battle for Mortain the fog lifted, exposing the Germans to attack by P-47s and RAF Typhoons. The airmen helped to dramatically decrease the numbers of enemy tanks. But this sort of close air support had its drawbacks. With German armor throughout the 30th's front lines, tanks from both sides were the target of air strikes. Friendly fire from the air and the ground became a common occurrence.

By evening the forward elements of 30th Division on Hill 314 near Mortain were surrounded and quickly became known to journalists as the Lost Battalion.[46] The 743d's Assault Gun Platoon fired 105 mm shells packed with medical supplies onto the hill to aid the besieged troops. The missions were fired at five-minute intervals to allow the troops time to spot the shells. Medical rounds continued to be fired on August 8 and 9. Morphine to ease the suffering of the wounded was urgently needed but the fragile ampoules were bursting on impact.

Its rear deck stacked with plasma, Cock Perry Kelly's tank worked its way through pockets of German soldiers to the battalion's Assault Gun Platoon. The tank arrived after dark and the precious cargo was unloaded, ready to be placed into the shells being fired onto Hill 314. The crew relocated their tank to await morning light before attempting the return trip. Cock climbed out from his forward hatch and moved cautiously through the darkness down a slope to a nearby stream. He filled his precious coffee pot with water, and, after returning, made coffee for everyone—a regular before-dinner ritual. Early the next morning Cock returned from the stream, empty pot in hand after discovering that strewn along the banks, and floating in the waters were the bodies of Germans killed during the previous days' battles.

On July 8 Dog Company left its defensive positions around the 30th Division's CP to participate with A Company in an attack on Romagny. An enemy counterattack temporarily stalled the A Company medium tanks paralleling D Company's advance. The fifteen tanks of Able Company split into two forces, one attacking towards Romagny, the second towards Mortain. The Mortain force intercepted an enemy armored column consisting of nine tanks. While the battle was under way, friendly aircraft set two A Company tanks ablaze and killed one crewman.[47]

Although Allied air superiority had greatly reduced the armored threat, isolated pockets of Germans stubbornly held their ground.

John Shanafelt was serving as liaison officer to the 30th Infantry Division when he transferred to 1st Platoon, Charlie Company. Shortly afterwards 1st Platoon was ordered to outflank German positions around Mortain. Shanafelt guided his new platoon downhill into a valley, unaware that their advance had been observed by German tankers. The platoon was stopped beside a hedgerow to await further instructions when suddenly exploding 88s shook the air and sent dark-colored cones of earth skyward.

When the barrage was over nobody seemed to be hurt. Then I saw one of the guys over there saying he was hit. He had been sitting there and shrapnel had struck him between the legs cutting two arteries. He bled to death in a matter of seconds.

We had been instructed to follow the road down to where a B Company tank had been hit and then take a left up the valley where the enemy was supposed to be. What nobody knew was that the British had been given instructions to attack anything in the valley that moved. Nobody was supposed to be there except Germans.[48]

After changing position, Shanafelt's platoon discovered that they were now above the road the German tanks were using to move toward them.

We were feeling pretty good about this whole deal because of our tactical advantage. We were moving into position to open fire when we were hit by our own aircraft. The rockets of friendly RAF Typhoons quickly set two tanks ablaze. Then as we tried to escape the flames, friendly artillery, undoubtedly signaled by the action of the planes, started smashing into us and the surrounding area.

We immediately moved to an orchard and into some outbuildings there to get under cover. The Germans went by and onto the next hill only to get clobbered by the next wave of aircraft. At that point we didn't know what the setup was.

Shanafelt took his gunner and crossed the road by foot.

From our hedgerow, one long field up, we could see a bunch of Jerries moving around and talking. So we returned to our tanks and waited. Later, hearing the engines of vehicles we remounted, assuming the Jerries had moved out. With one man gut shot, I ordered a German captured earlier to load our two dead onto the back of the tank. Then I led the column on foot back up the road to where we expected to run into our troops and we did. That was my first day in combat.

Less than three miles away, Baker Company was attempting to move to Barenton when mines blew the tracks off one tank. Barenton had been reported as "liberated," but B Company tankers were forced to take up positions a mile from the village as they repulsed two enemy counterattacks.[49]

The following day, German counterattacks were so intense that no help was available when A Company called for more infantry support. By the end of the afternoon two tankers had been killed, and four others were missing in action.

In an attempt to break the German line at Romagny, B Company left their positions outside Barenton and moved to Fontenay to join A and C Companies' continuing assault. Two attacks were made, neither were successful. In this action three men were wounded in their turrets by sniper fire; two others were also wounded and three listed as missing in action when their tank burned.[50] From somewhere in front the direct fire of an 88 was wreaking havoc on the Shermans. Moments later another tank was hit, and only two crewmen escaped the flames. Immediately after, a nearby dozer tank that had just successfully set fire to a German tank was also struck. Fortunately, the crewmen of the dozer were able to evacuate without casualties. The fire fights of August 10, the fourth day of battle, marked the beginning of the cleanup action.

On August 12, five days after Von Rundstedt's Mortain offensive began, Baker Company, flanked by two files of Old Hickory's 30th Division infantry, moved into Mortain. Behind were the A Company tanks that were to pass through the town and out the other side to pursue and harass retreating German infantry.

Spaced thirty yards apart, Able Company's 3d Platoon rolled cautiously into heavily bombed Mortain. Tank tracks clacked noisily down ruined vacant streets bordered by teetering remnants of masonry walls firmly rooted in deep rubble moraines.

The tanks moved down the ruined streets between rows of ruined houses, then slowly rounded a corner. In turn, each driver jerked back on the lever controlling the right track, holding it in place while the left track spun the tank around the curve. The last tank in line, George Johnson reached for the power traverse lever to rotate the turret to the rear. With the possibility of heavy German armor lurking in the ruins the last tank in any group was just as important as the first. At the same time Johnson's driver braked the right-track lever, and the tank began to move around the curve in quick jerky motions. The driver saved the lives of the crew as two rockets loosed by a British Typhoon blasted the rubble strewn street to either side of the tank. The twin explosions rocked the tank and sent black smoke billowing up through every crevice in the hull, filling the inside with the odor of explosives.

Damaged but drivable the tank pulled out of line and started slowly back down the road that led into town. It was along this lane that a crewless Sherman M4, its engines idling, was spotted in an adjacent field. The commander dismounted, walked to the tank, then drove it out to the road. After transferring their gear, the crew turned up the lane to Mortain.

While the 30th Division and 743d tankers were embroiled in continuous battle around Mortain, Patton's Third Army had swung around toward Argentan to link with the British and Canadians pushing down from Caumont and Caen. When the two forces joined, the remnants of the Germans' Seventh Army were trapped in the "Falaise pocket," 300 square miles of Norman territory.

On the fifth day, following the start of their counterattack, the Germans' Mortain-Avranches push was an acknowledged failure. Hans Speidel later recorded that the counteroffensive had simply wasted German Panzer forces south of the Seine and was "contrary to the laws of strategy as well as to common sense . . . an unexpected gift of decisive value to the enemy."[51]

Stretched to the limit in officers, men and material the two-month long Norman campaign provided the 743d with innumerable valuable lessons for tank-infantry coordination, communications, field improvements to armor and stalking tactics to be used when confronted with the heavier and better gunned Panther and Tiger tanks. It was also learned that the long-barreled 76 mm gun was preferable to the short-barreled low velocity 75 mm. In response to the enormous losses of his crews and tanks Colonel Duncan tried to obtain replacement medium tanks outfitted with the 76 mm. Duncan was informed that no such weapons were available because every tank coming ashore in France with a 76 mm main gun had been requested by General Patton.[52]

The Norman countryside had tested the 743d under some of the worst battle and weather conditions then imaginable. The results showed that the 743d veterans were equal to their German counterparts. With the encirclement of the German Seventh Army at Falaise, the 743d began the rat race to the north and east.

IV

In a Field Near La Glieze

IT IS AXIOMATIC IN THE ART OF WAR THAT THE SIDE WHICH REMAINS BEHIND
ITS FORTIFIED LINE IS ALWAYS DEFEATED.

Napoleon 1793

THE GREAT BATTLE OF AACHEN

Following the encirclement of the German 7th Army in the
Falaise Gap, Allied forces in Western France began a rapid drive
east to Paris and north to Belgium, Holland, and Germany. The
battalion's entry into Germany would be marked by the same slow-
moving, difficult battles familiar from Normandy where territorial
gains were often measured in mere yards.

Released from the confines of the Norman *bocage*, the 743d's
tanks, trucks and other vehicles pursued the fleeing German army
northwards.[1] The tankers encountered token German rear guard
action along roadways littered with discarded and destroyed
equipment. The columns sped through the French countryside and
crawled through crowded village streets where the young and old
passed up gifts of fruit, wine, and hard cider to the tankers. The
battalion had its first glimpse of Paris during the pursuit north
when the top of the Eiffel tower was spied on the horizon.[2] The
rapid advance slowed briefly at the banks of the Seine River, then
regained its momentum only to be hobbled by inadequate fuel
supplies.

All along their road march, the 743d acquired first-hand
evidence of the effectiveness and willingness of the Free French
Forces to participate in their liberation and to implement their own

quick justice. One individual who has remained particularly fresh in the memories of Able Company veterans was an unnamed young man between nineteen and twenty-two years of age. The lean, dark-haired youth, furnished with a helmet, uniform, and a tanker's Thompson machine gun, had proved himself time and time again as the company's scout, interpreter, guide, and fellow combatant. From southwest of Paris to the German border the youth repeatedly took risks others couldn't or wouldn't. Upon reaching the German frontier, A Company tankers decided that it was time to legitimize their friendship with the youth by making him a member of the American army. Besides, it had become far too difficult to disguise their friend from Headquarters personnel because he often rode astride the 75 mm barrels of the company's various tanks. Nonetheless, efforts to join him with the unit failed, not because of his nationality nor his incredible record of combat experience, but simply because all members of the armed forces had to be physically fit, and the youth had only one leg.[3]

On September 2, near Tournai, the 743d Tank Battalion became the first American armor to enter Belgium; in a week's time, Battalion tanks were approaching Holland's famous Fort Eben Emael. Two days later, Charlie Company's 1st Platoon crossed into Mheer, Holland, becoming the first Americans to enter that country.

The 30th Division's dash towards northern Germany slowed when American forces met their enemy along the Maas or Meuse River in the Netherlands' panhandle separating Germany and Belgium. Five days after battalion tanks reached the border of Hitler's Reich, enemy forces made a desperate attempt to slow the advancing infantry and armor. German artillery fire herded Dutch men, women, children, the handicapped and the ill of the town of Kerkrade towards the Americans. By nightfall, 30,000 to 35,000 civilians were being housed and fed in makeshift quarters immediately behind the American front.[4]

The 30th's defensive line stretched between the Dutch "panhandle towns" of Maastricht, Valkenberg, and Heerlen. Preparations were quickly made to enter Germany, and on September 19, 743d Able Company tankers were alongside Old Hickory infantrymen at Scherpenseel.[5] Behind, less than 150 miles away to the west, Dunkerque was still under German control.

The Dutch panhandle cuts roughly 30 miles southward between Belgium and Germany, barely 10 miles wide at some points. The handle separates Liege from Aachen, Brussels from Cologne, and Antwerp from Düsseldorf, and stops in the south where low hills mark the northern limits of the Ardennes. The Maas River meanders from one side of the panhandle to the other. Fewer than

80 miles to the east is the Roer River and the mining and industrial center of the Ruhr.

In under three months' time the Americans and their Allies had penetrated the Atlantic Wall and sat poised to cross the German border defenses known as the West Wall—referred to among American troops as the Siegfried Line—stretching from the Dutch border southeast towards Switzerland. The battles of October sought to breach the West Wall defenses, to take Aachen, the largest German city in the 30th's sector, and to move on to the Roer. The battle for Aachen and access to the Roer continued for eight long weeks. The Germans' last major counteroffensive in the west ended the Siegfried Line Campaign when it broke through Allied defenses in the Ardennes.

From the German point of view, this sequence of events is known as the Great Battle of Aachen.[6] Set within the defenses of the West Wall, Aachen is approximately six miles from the Dutch town of Kerkrade and possessed greater symbolic than strategic importance for the German state. Aachen had been one of the most important of the political and religious sites of the ninth-century Emperor Charlemagne. The spiritual and political seat of the First Reich could not be left undefended.

Although the defenses of the West Wall continued over terrain as varied as conifer forests and coal mines, the landscape in front of the 30th was largely agricultural, spotted with villages set against a horizon line softened by stands of gray, leafless trees. The most visible element contributing to the West Wall defensive system was the so-called Dragons' Teeth. These artificial tank obstacles consisted of truncated concrete pyramids set in rows four or five deep, increasing in height from a little over two feet in the front to as much as five feet high in the back.[7] Because the pyramids were cast as part of an interlocking grid of concrete beams, they proved nearly impossible to dislodge. Consequently, forced penetrations by vehicles were channeled through the heavily defended passageways, with their minefields, pillboxes, and casemates equipped with antitank guns located to provide mutual fire support.

Scheduled for October 2, the assault on the West Wall included crossing the Wurm River below the castle of Rimberg following an airstrike of over 400 medium and fighter bombers. Although the Wurm River was in many places barely 30 feet wide and 3 to 6 feet deep it had been purposely enlarged, and so this artificially exaggerated stream became a large muddy tank ditch. In the farmland to either side of the crossing site there was little natural or artificial cover. Therefore, during the pre-assault planning it was agreed that the tankers would only be called either to cross or to provide direct fire support for infantry.

On the morning of October 2, fewer than a dozen planes hit the target area. Most bombs were either too short or too long, although the fighter bombers did manage to hit the area with napalm-like jelly fire bombs.

At midday, contrary to the agreement, an infantry lieutenant colonel called for Able Company tankers too early. Upon their arrival, much like what had occurred at the beach exits of Omaha, the tanks attracted even more enemy artillery, making it doubly difficult for the engineers building temporary bridges. Unable to return to their staging area the Shermans crashed off the roadway and into the muddy, cratered farmland to sit for four hours amidst the continuous explosions of German artillery.[8] Their luck held until late in the afternoon when just prior to crossing, an artillery shell struck the turret of the company commander's tank, wounding him and his cannoneer. The next day, shortly after crossing at the Rimberg location, five of ten Charlie Company tanks bogged down in the mud as did the two T-2 recovery vehicles sent out to help. The occasionally heavy autumn rainfall aggravated the tankers in their narrow-tracked Shermans. Muddied fields were impassable, and without adequate mine clearing equipment, even well-maintained roads could be difficult, slow travelling for the tankers whose role it was to propel the desired advances.

The contest between American and German artillerymen continued through the night and into the next day when the 2d Armored Division crossed the Wurm and became entangled in Old Hickory's road net. At the same time the Germans began a nearly continuous series of counterattacks. These counterattacks were most often made up of large numbers of troops supported by limited numbers of tanks. The largest counterattack against the Rimberg bridgehead came on the fourth day of battle at 7 A.M. and lasted eight hours. At the end of the day the major part of the bridgehead ground had been retaken, although isolated elements of the German assault force were still holding out in their recaptured pillboxes.[9] Some of the German infantry were so well emplaced that tank commanders resorted to driving up to slit trenches to lob hand grenades from their turrets.[10]

The following morning, 743d tanks consolidated the crossing site when they led an attack south to capture Wilhelmschacht and Alsdorf over roadways heavily sown with booby traps and mines. Its river passage secured, the 30th could now push towards Aachen and an eventual linkup with 1st Division infantry.

The Germans met the American threat to Aachen with everything available, including reserves brought in from as far away as Arnhem, Holland, and Luxembourg.[11] On October 12, under cover of an early morning fog, these forces made an all-out attack on the front line northeast of Wurselen at Birk. Melvin Beiber's lone Baker Company tank was caught by the main blow of the assault. Suddenly, Beiber's crew was battling a Mark V Panther and Mark VI Tiger at the same time. After using 12 hits to destroy the Panther, Beiber's crew concentrated rapid fire on the Tiger to force its retreat.[12]

743d tankers demonstrated unwavering tenacity, as on a previous occasion when direct fire destroyed four tanks of A Company's 3d Platoon, leaving only one tank operational. The surviving crewmen gathered available weapons and began fighting as infantry alongside the remaining tank.[13]

To overcome the West Wall, the battalion worked their tanks around to the entrances of the successive fortified positions and used a shell of HE to blow it open, or resorted to using their new flame-throwing tanks. If a position couldn't be destroyed, dozer tanks sealed it with earth. During this time the German units defending the border continued to reap their harvest. The battalion lost 22 tanks during the close-in fighting, but were able to claim 18 German tanks including three Mark VI Tiger Royals. During these fire-fights between ill-matched tanks the sandbagging sometimes staved off immediate disaster. On October 10, for instance, Sergeant Alvin Tisland's tank suffered three hits by direct fire, but he and his crew continued to fight until disabled by a shot-off track.[14]

The battalion's quick thrusts into the countryside bordering the Wurm River held the danger of battlefield isolation. Two remarkable incidents illustrate the oftentimes precarious situation of the tankers.

While leading an attack just two miles north of Aachen, Lieutenant Don Mason's Able Company tank A13—a D-Day survivor—became isolated between the two forces in no man's land. Behind the tank the unsuccessful attack had halted, leaving the crew to fend for itself. For two days the five men held off successive counterattacks by Tiger and Panther tanks before the front line caught up again. A few days later a Panzer brigade consisting of 30 tanks and infantry in half-tracks counterattacked the battalion. Sergeant Earnest Kirksey's Baker Company tank was confronted by nine enemy tanks at close range. Before help arrived Kirksey's crew fired 60 rounds in 15 minutes, destroying one of the bigger German battle tanks and causing the others to halt.[15] Such episodes illustrate the value and cool application of training and experience and the knowledge that even a 75 mm can kill a Tiger at 100 yards or less.[16]

On yet another occasion direct fire disabled an A Company tank, stranding the survivors at a nearby farmstead. Perry "Cock" Kelly went forward with his tank "King Cock" and discovered the men beside a farmhouse below a gully. Kelly's crew had unwittingly entered a trap. Distant buildings concealed Panther Mark V and Tiger Mark VI tanks, which now resumed their direct fire. Kelly's driver quickly moved "King Cock" behind the barn. The crew sat with hatches tightly closed as the Germans lobbed shells over the building trying to find their target. The men watched the barnyard chickens through the thick lens of their periscopes. At first they seemed to be unperturbed by the shelling. Then a round exploded directly over the barnyard. When the dust cleared, featherless chickens were stumbling drunkenly about until each collapsed from the concussion.

The crew sat behind the barn for several days using hay and other material to further camouflage the tank from intermittent blasts. During this time a Missing in Action notice was sent to the home of Kelly's mother in Washington state. Shortly after, the tankers made radio contact with division artillerymen.

The standoff ended when the Panther tank drove down the road and parked opposite some trees screening the farmyard. Incredibly, a crewman got out and began to relieve himself. Perry's crew fired six AP rounds all of which ricocheted off the Mark V. While firing, contact was made with a forward artillery observer and the tank was disabled.

Rejoined with A Company Kelly was about to make coffee when he received the order to move out. At that moment Cock discovered his Norman coffee pot had been forgotten at the farmyard.

By the middle of the second week of October, Aachen was nearly enveloped. A 2,000 to 3,000-yard hole in the front lines separated the 30th (of the XIX Corps, Ninth Army) and First Infantry Divisions (of the VII Corps, First Army). American attacks to close what quickly became known as the Aachen Gap started on the 13th of October, continued on the 14th, and stalemated at Wurselen on the 15th. The entire 60th Panzer Grenadier Regiment using dug-in tanks supported by engineer and reconnaissance battalions was stubbornly defending Wurselen.[17] Attacks on Aachen were further complicated by bad weather, which prevented airstrikes and grounded the artillery observation planes used to spot enemy assembly areas.

Until October 15, the tactical preference had been for a push southward towards Aachen, behind, or more correctly *within*, the defenses of the West Wall. This tactic was seen as less difficult than recrossing the Wurm farther south and confronting West Wall strongpoints with a frontal assault. There were no signs, however, of any weakening resistance in Wurselen's buildings and streets where the stiff opposition was well supported by German artillery.[18] The Wurselen stalemate forced the 30th to attempt a new attack southwards between the city and the Wurm River which was to be coordinated with a crossriver attack. The new strategy proved successful and late on the evening of October 16 troops of the 30th and 1st Divisions made contact. Although the Aachen gap had been closed and Charlemagne's capitol was under siege, there were continuous attacks on the former gap by German troops and tanks seeking to escape encirclement, some of which were successful. Aachen surrendered on October 21 after 5 days of bitter street warfare. Wurselen, on the other hand, remained a vital part of the Germans' defensive line until three weeks later when the town was itself threatened with encirclement. It was at that moment and under cover of night that the remnants of the German force withdrew.[19]

Throughout the push into Germany the 743d and the 30th Infantry Division reaped the benefits of a refinement in tank-infantry coordination first implemented in Normandy. This improvement consisted of dividing the 743d Headquarters Staff into three advance sub-command posts, each associated with one of the three infantry regiments of the 30th Infantry Division.[20] On November 22 the close association of command elements produced an impressive reward when the 120th Infantry Regiment, supported by 743d tanks, overran five villages and pushed to within four miles of the Roer River. The combined infantry-tank action was so successful that it was later reenacted for replacement 30th Division officers.[21]

The attack began under the rain. Battalion-sized groups of infantry, supported by tanks, attacked and held an objective, after which a second group attacked through the first unit's position. This was followed by a third force attacking through the position held by the second unit. This pattern of operations kept the enemy off guard and under constant attack while allowing successive groups to reorganize and resupply before reattacking. That morning, tanks and infantry leapfrogged through the towns of Lurken and Langweiler, and later Laurensberg and Obermerz.[22] In the afternoon the leapfrogging units continued to Fronhoven and Langendorf.

Five days after Thanksgiving, P-47s strafed the battalion's positions in the village of Langendorf. To help the pilots avoid further mistakes, an antiaircraft unit, located in a field beside the town, sent up a yellow signal flare. When the planes continued circling, the battalion's five assault guns quickly laid yellow identification panels on their rear engine decks. Within seconds of laying out the panels the P-47s bombed all the well marked positions. By the time the pilots had departed, there were eight casualties including one death.[23]

The attacks into Germany that had started with the West Wall culminated with an unusually easy assault on the towns of Pattern and Kol Kellersberg near the Roer River. Baker Company tanks began firing onto one side of Pattern while a column of A Company tanks roared down a side road into town. Suddenly, the tanks leading the pincer movement found themselves behind two Panzerjäger Panthers (assault guns mounted on Panther chassis) distracted by B Company's diversion. The Shermans knocked out both vehicles through their thin side armor at between 50 and 75 yards. The tankers continued farther into town where they discovered a third Panzerjäger Panther hidden in an alley. Able Company tanks took a position 100 yards opposite the building hiding the Panther and used a round of H.E. to blast a hole through the structure, quickly followed by another round sent into the German tank.

Three months after attacking the West Wall the Americans had penetrated only twenty-two miles into Germany.[24] The German soldiers occupying the West Wall defenses had fought an effective delaying action while preparing for a massive counteroffensive farther south.

When December began in Pattern and Kol Kellersberg, the battalion's numerous replacements were busy training in radio, map reading, tank tactics, weapons maintenance, and instruction in the use of the newly installed gyro stabilizer. Recently introduced from stateside, the gyro aided the positioning and firing of the Sherman's 75 mm gun while the tank was under way. Although the gyro may have been of some use in division-level tank warfare, the best shot remained that fired from a stationary position in the close-in combat experienced by 743d tankers.[25]

More practical and welcome innovations were arriving from the states. Service Company mechanics outfitted the battalion's assault guns and the tank dozers of Charlie Company with new "Duckbill" tread extenders. These distributed the tank's ground weight more evenly and increased off-road traction in muddy terrain. Eleven A Company tanks equipped with a new secret weapon, the T-22 rocket launcher, were also being readied. The menacing-looking turret-mounted rockets were to supplement the battalion's flame thrower tanks. Elsewhere maintenance crews welded brackets onto the newly arrived M4A3 and M4A1 model tanks to hold the lifesaving layers of sandbags. As the date for crossing the Roer River neared, each tank was loaded with 15 rounds of HE-AT and 25 rounds of "Block Buster."[26]

The cold and humid winter days of northern Germany wore on until the end of the first week of December, when cooler weather brought in a snowstorm. On the 11th the weather temporarily changed back to rain, but by mid-month winter set in for good with temperatures that left the ground firmly frozen in the mornings.

Battalion battle readiness was often signaled by the issuance of furloughs, and now men began receiving 48-hour passes to Kerkrade, Holland. In addition, two hundred battalion personnel attended a December 14 dance at the Limburgia Cafe in Heerlen, Holland. The men enjoyed civilian food, the company of 80 English-speaking dance club hostesses, and the swing music of the 66th Air Ground Forces dance band.[27] Less pleasurable were the 1 to 2 hour conditioning hikes, principally by the tankers of the line companies, to shake the growing lethargy of the quasi-normal camp life. The comfortable self-confident atmosphere evaporated when news reached the 743d of Von Rundstedt's thrust through the American VIII Corps zone in the Belgian Ardennes, just south of the battalion. The Allies' headlong rush to Berlin halted and the preparations for the Roer River attack were set aside as a new set of anxieties took their place. The battalion received orders to move south under cover of darkness beginning on the following day.

DOWN TO THE BULGE

WE HAD NO MAPS TO FOLLOW, WE WERE JUST TOLD TO GO UNTIL YOU MEET THE GERMANS.

Harlan Whitcomb, C Company[28]

On the afternoon of December 16 men on pass were rounded up, and the assault gun crews exchanged their ammunition so that the 105 mm guns could operate as tanks instead of artillery. The move took the tankers back through Aachen and south into the area of the Belgian Ardennes located at the bottom of the Dutch panhandle. The departure was awaited sleeplessly in part because enemy planes were heavily bombing the battalion's front lines. During the night the light tanks of Dog Company were sent to Bardenburg to round up German paratroopers that had been part of a diversionary force.[29]

The next day under cover of rain and darkness the battalion made its road march into the heart of the German counteroffensive one mile north of Malmedy, Belgium. The 743d was joining an Allied force preparing to hit the German bulge from three sides. First Army was striking from the north, Third Army from the south and a British Corps was attacking from the west.

One tank after another wound over the dark roads. Drivers strained their eyes to see the twin-glowing red slits of the tail lights on the tank in front. "Cateye" reflectors attached to the rear engine deck of each Sherman aided drivers struggling to maintain the required fifteen yards between tanks. The two reflectors looked like one when following at the correct distance, but shone separately when too close. When first introduced, a popular rumor circulated alleging that cateyes were manufactured from a substance that could render an individual sterile if carried in a pant pocket. Undoubtedly designed to keep the reflectors in active use, the rumor backfired, and everyone wanted to carry a set of his own.[30]

Throughout the drive south behind the long American front line, the aerial activity was intensive, the flak and antiaircraft (AA) fire almost continuous on both sides of the road. It was difficult and tiring driving in column in the night, sometimes under rain, sometimes over roads worn dry and dusty by the constant passage of vehicles. The nerves of crewmen were strained further by warnings to be on the lookout for additional enemy paratroopers. 1st Lieutenant Joseph Couri recalled:

> . . . if the fumes, dirt, rocks and the roar of the tank engines were not enough, we had to contend with enemy flares being dropped throughout the march, our antiaircraft guns and tracer bullets putting them out, and the drone of the enemy aircraft above. Also the Buzz-Bombs were going overhead all night long heading for Liege. I was still trying to figure out what they were. . . . My eyes were red, swollen and irritated from the grime and dust traveling behind another tank at close quarters with the turret open and standing all the time.[31]

The heavily forested, hilly country of the Ardennes opened a new chapter in the combat experience of the 743d. Open terrain—tank country—was confined primarily to fields or areas bordering roads and towns. Secondary roads and the raw unimproved firebreaks cutting through the forests were often little wider than two tanks. Even in dry summer weather the thick forests blanketing the hilly terrain blocked the passage of most vehicles and confined battles to short cross country attacks and road-based advances.[32]

At the outset, Von Rundstedt's winter offensive benefited from several advantages. The first was the weather and terrain. The second was the recent arrival in the Ardennes of an uninitiated outfit fresh from stateside and two American divisions badly injured in the battles of the Huertgen Forest.[33]

Once the German march through the Ardennes stalled, crossroads (much like what the battalion had experienced in Normandy) provided the enemy with ideal strong points allowing serial defensive options. Denied an easy escape, the heavy German armor was often employed in static defense positions. The Germans typically kept one route for withdrawal and all the others were defended. American attacks began at the edge of villages from where the Germans would be pushed back through the constricted streets, past spacious town squares, and then once again into narrower streets until reaching the other side of town. Again and again in Stoumont, Stavelot, and Thirimont the Germans repeated this effective defensive pattern. When confronting unusually stubborn German roadblocks 743d tankers discovered that the deep snow-covered fields required the infantry to attempt flanking movements without their armored support.

The tactics learned by the battalion in the towns and countryside around Malmedy would be the same encountered after crossing the Roer. Through it all, the lack of specialized mine-clearing equipment slowed and endangered the tankers and accompanying doughs.

Upon his arrival at Malmedy Colonel Duncan learned that the town was in the heart of the sector through which the 1st SS Panzer Division, *Leibstandarte Adolf Hitler*, was attempting to drive on through to Liege, Belgium. After meeting with the CO of the 117th Infantry Regiment, Colonel Duncan gathered his tank platoon leaders at a high point north of town with the one available map. No one knew more than another, and questions as to where the enemy was located were responded to by "The front is fluid."[34] Duncan deployed the 743d along a line stretching approximately five miles with the forward command post at Malmedy. The rest of the administrative elements were lodged at Xhoffraix. Duncan's plan called for Able Company to remain in Malmedy attached to the 3d Battalion 117th Infantry Regiment. Baker Company, with the exception of 3d Platoon, went to join the 2d Battalion of the 117th in the vicinity of Masta. 3d Platoon, along with three of the battalion's assault guns, was allocated to the 1st Battalion 117th Infantry at Stavelot. Available Charlie Company tanks joined the 119th Infantry at Stoumont.[35]

The line companies moved out with assignments in hand. Despite all the care and careful maintenance given the tanks at Pattern and Kol Kellersberg, the overnight road march brought forth additional maintenance problems. Soon tanks B17 and B19, of B Company's 3d Platoon, dropped out for repairs, a significant loss when facing German armor. The three remaining tanks and three assault guns continued to Stavelot.

The Buzz Bombs seen and heard by the 743d as they moved to the Bulge had been destined for the Belgian city of Liege. Liege had been the initial objective of the tanks of the 1st SS Division Adolf Hitler under command of Colonel Peiper. Peiper's troops were now intractably mired in the bulge they had helped to create in the American front line.

After being injured during one of the Buzz Bomb raids, Anny Maertins de Noordhout and her family left Liege to live with family members at Stavelot—unwittingly moving directly into the path of the oncoming German forces. On the second day of the offensive, Anny and others watched as American troops retreated through the village.

Early the next morning the family counted sixty big German tanks coming down the hill into town. It was the 1st SS Division Adolf Hitler commanded by Colonel Peiper. The tanks were rumbling past where Anny and her family were staying when two shells hit the house. It was so badly damaged they had to leave it. They crept out of the house by the back door, down a narrow street to a house of an aunt who had died sometime before. They stayed there until about five o'clock in the evening when they realized the roof of the house was burning. . . . the SS had set fire to four houses because the street was too narrow for their huge tanks. The seven adults and four children again moved. There was one more relative's house they could go to but it stood directly across the town square from where they were. An American tank and German tank stood at opposite corners of the square, [in between lay] dead civilians and soldiers. . . . Anny and her group decided the best way would be to walk directly across the open area where they could be seen. They thought if they tried to sneak around the backs of the houses, either side could mistake them for the enemy and try to shoot them. Suddenly, as they began across the square they heard a voice cry out in German "Halt, kinder kinder!" The shooting stopped for the children. When they were safely inside the house the shooting began again. The German tank was blown up and all inside it were killed.[36]

3d Platoon arrived at Stavelot and learned that half of the town was firmly in the hands of the 1st SS Panzer Division under the command of Colonel Peiper. The platoon, operating with only three tanks, established defensive positions on the southeast side of the town square alongside doughs already in place there. One man was left on guard while the rest of the crew dismounted and

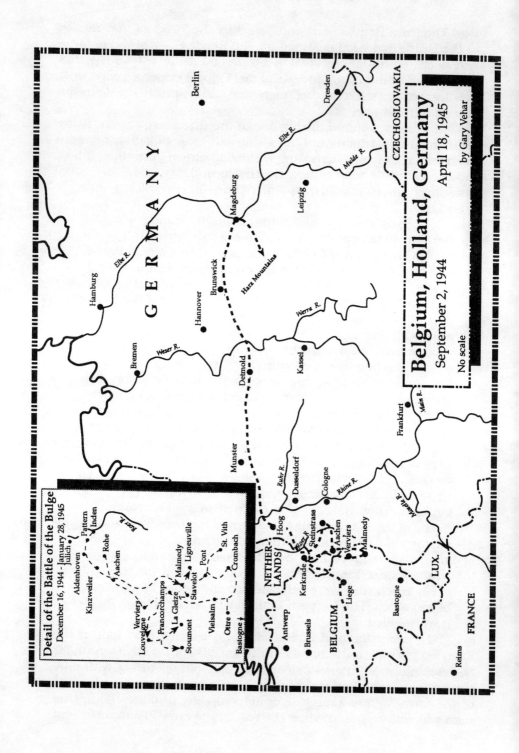

Belgium, Holland, Germany
September 2, 1944 — April 18, 1945
by Gary Vehar
No scale

Detail of the Battle of the Bulge
December 16, 1944 - January 28, 1945

began setting up living quarters in a nearby house. The battalion's assault gun crews took up firing positions just outside town. The reinforcement was timely.

Four hours after their arrival two trucks loaded with German infantry attacked across the town square. Sergeant Kirksey and a dough acting as sentries didn't have time to do more than return small arms fire but they caught the Germans unaware and stopped their drive fifteen feet short of Kirksey's tank, B16. The two men were speedily joined by others and both German vehicles were disabled, one soldier was killed, and the remainder forced to withdraw to their own line, a scant 70 yards away.

Brought back to their tanks by the brief fire fight, the crews were better prepared when within ten minutes, another truck tried to attack across the square. This time, tank B15 bucked as a round of HE from its main gun destroyed the truck while the assistant driver's .30 caliber chased the remaining Germans out of the square.[37]

The 743d medium tank jerkily moved into the open. Staff Sergeant Howard Froberg took up a new position in front of the house with the children, moving his crew into the main floor of the dwelling and the family into the basement. At least dry and warm quarters were close at hand.

While 3d Platoon held its ground in Stavelot, Baker Company's 2d Platoon and two of the battalion's assault guns arrived in Masta. Because Headquarters expected Masta to be another hot spot, B Company's 1st Platoon tanks were also sent to join the defenders. However, as had happened so often in the past, the heat came from the sky when "friendly" P-47s strafed the tankers' positions. No one was hurt, but there was a good scare when a bullet from one of the aircraft's .50 caliber machine guns ricocheted wildly inside the turret of one tank.[38]

Early in the morning of December 18 the remainder of C and D Companies arrived from Germany. Charlie Company's 3d Platoon departed immediately for Chevron with the 2d Battalion of the 119th Infantry while 1st and 2d Platoons deployed with the 3d Battalion of the 119th Infantry Regiment at Stoumont. The following day Stoumont and Stavelot felt the full fury of an all out attack by German veterans of the Russian front.

Heavy artillery fire shattered the quiet winter morning in Stavelot, presaging a series of counterattacks by Peiper's armored SS troops. Faced with the threat of being overrun, the three assault gun crews began using their 105 mm guns for direct fire, destroying or disabling five vehicles in the German armored column. In response, the German artillery supporting the attack tried to zero in on the assault gun positions. When the crews realized this, they began firing a few rounds in quick succession before moving their guns and firing again. Stymied in their attempt to destroy the guns, the German artillerymen began using air bursts over the assault gun crews and 3d Platoon tanks in an effort to isolate them from their infantry.

When 1st Lieutenant Walter Macht arrived in the nearby village of Stoumont, he arranged C Company's 1st Platoon alongside troops already dug in on the high ground at the eastern edge of town. 2d Platoon set up road blocks inside town.[39] It was almost 7A.M. and the new arrivals didn't have long to wait.

Within fifteen minutes the Germans attacked from the south and east with almost 40 tanks plus a battalion of infantry mounted on half-tracks. A three-hour-long fight began with heavy mortars, automatic weapons, small arms and point-blank tank fire. C Company gunner Corporal Harlan Whitcomb recalled:

> We were greatly outnumbered, so we had to retreat. Our tank was sitting at the end of the street. Our Tank Commander got out to look around. While he was gone I saw a German tank starting to pull out in the street about a block away. As the tank turned and faced down the street I fired an armor piercing shell into him, [then] I didn't see any movement from the German tank, nor did he fire back. I was looking straight down his barrel. By this time the Tank Commander had returned and we retreated down the street past an antiaircraft 90mm gun and crew. Just as we passed them they fired at something that I could not see. We set up a road block just beyond this gun.[40]

As the battle progressed it became necessary to withdraw towards Targnon to prevent being overwhelmed by the sheer numbers of German heavy battle tanks. The infantry began fighting from house to house, slowly and carefully withdrawing north and west under the tanks' intense covering fire. To provide additional time for the reorganization of a new firing line, the retreating infantry scattered mines in the path of their attackers.

Caught by the center of the German blow, 2d Platoon knocked out three enemy tanks and two half-tracks, substantially slowing the mechanized team advancing from the east. At the same instant 1st Platoon tanks knocked out two more German tanks and a half-track, thereby stalling the advance from the south.

When 1st Platoon tanks began their withdrawal, the remaining riflemen climbed on the rear engine decks. With 1st Platoon disengaged, 2d Platoon began pulling back, tank by tank, all the while exchanging direct fire with the oncoming German heavy tanks.[41]

Macht redeployed at the new defensive line set up along a ravine above a bend in the road outside town. The German attack stopped to allow removal of the hastily laid mines. By the time the enemy armored column appeared at the bend, much needed ammo and reinforcements were arriving at the new emplacement. Tank C10 knocked out the lead enemy tank at under 500 yards, inspiring the remainder of the enemy column to withdraw around the safety of the corner. The big German tanks dispersed into the forest from where they continued intermittent direct fire. When the column tried sending a 150 mm self-propelled gun around the corner, 1st Platoon tanks destroyed it also. Winter's dusk was hurriedly bringing darkness and the action was the last for the afternoon. The day long battle in Stoumont had cost 3d Battalion over 200 men and most of its heavy equipment.

1st and 2d Platoon tanks withdrew that same evening to Ruy and joined the 2d Battalion 120th Infantry. While pulling back, three tanks were temporarily left under guard in Remonchamps due to a lack of fuel and maintenance problems, and another tank was completely lost when it slid off an icy bridge and overturned into the freezing waters of the Spa River. One crew member was killed and a second injured in the accident; among the tankers it was the first death of the day.

While B and C Companies battled for their positions in Stavelot and Stoumont, the situation in Malmedy remained quiet. So quiet in fact that the regimental commander of the 117th Infantry requested that Colonel Duncan's Able Company accompany his 3d Battalion to Francorchamps and southwest down the valley toward a village named La Glieze (less than two miles direct distance from Stoumont) in hopes of driving the enemy south.[42] By midafternoon of December 19, A Company tanks and the trucks carrying the infantrymen had worked their way to Roanne and the enemy.

Joseph Couri's 2d Platoon and Floyd Jenkins' 3d Platoon, both of A Company, had just passed through Ruy and were approaching the junction with the Cour-Spa road when the infantry spotted movement up ahead.

> Our column halted as patrols were sent out and we were happy to find that a makeshift unit consisting of two 90mm AA guns, a few half-tracks and assault guns were defending this junction and also Gas Dump No. 2 with 2,000,000 gallons of gas along the road leading to Spa only some three hundred yards away.[43]

The battalion's Shermans were a welcome sight. Before long, German tanks began testing the defenses at the junction. The assault guns opened up just as the Germans started removing the mines blocking their passage up the road. The Germans returned fire, then retreated to the vicinity of Cour. Jenkins and Couri seized this opportunity to attack the village of Cour, forcing the Germans to retreat beyond Bourgamont. Couri recalled their next encounter with Colonel Peiper's 1st SS Panzer Division.

On December 20 early in the morning we jumped off for La Glieze. I was leading the task force in a dense fog almost impossible to see or fight in if one had to. We crept all the way to Bourgamont. The fog started to lift about nine o'clock. A few Belgian civilians came up the road from La Glieze and informed me and Lt. Jenkins what was ahead of us. On our area photo they pinpointed out the positions of the Germans between Bourgamont and La Glieze, [and] a roadblock set up a little to the distance from La Glieze; that was the news we did not want to hear.

At this very time, as we were preparing to advance, Colonel Duncan, our battalion commander, called me to say that the Third Armored Division arriving from the north was soon to pass through our lines and our taking of La Glieze was cancelled. And indeed the Third Armored came along at a good rate of speed. I stepped out on the road to flag them down and warn them of what was in their path.

While I was giving the information to the 1st Lieutenant of the lead platoon [sic] a Major arrived at the head of the column to find out why it had stopped. I was talking with the Lieutenant when he approached. The situation was explained to him and he said "Move out." Lt. Jenkins and I went over near [the major's] jeep where he was in contact with his Lieutenant. After about ten or twelve medium tanks went by we heard this volley of shots ring out throughout the valley. We knew what had happened and had heard it on the radio. The two lead tanks were destroyed by direct fire with most of the men killed or wounded. The column retreated and took up defensive positions; we did the same.[44]

The tankers had unwittingly run straight into the command post of the 1st SS Panzer Division and its main pocket of armor. After a second attack failed, Third Armor pulled back to try assaults from Stoumont and Stavelot. On the 21st, Able Company's 3d Platoon was erroneously attached to Third Armor and moved out with them for an attack on La Glieze. Pushed to the front to help lead the assault, the platoon's tanks were obliged to try a frontal attack on the well prepared German positions. Driving down the road from Bourgamont the tanks fired their main guns and machine guns while tank commanders heaved hand grenades and fired Tommyguns at the enemy infantry dug in along the roadside. Before long this third attack was turned back.[45] The fighting for La Glieze temporarily halted between December 20 and the 23d.

Able Company tanks continued holding their defensive positions at Bourgamont. During this time Gasoline Depot No. 2 was evacuated, but not before the Germans tried again to take the vital fuel reserves there by using the town of Bourgamont as a break-out route from the La Glieze pocket. On this occasion 743d tankers gave themselves the defensive advantage when Sergeant Jones concealed his tank at a spot overlooking the curve in the road leading from La Glieze to Bourgamont.

I was called back to the Infantry C.P. on the high ground north of Bourgamont overlooking the whole valley and a view of the road leading up from La Glieze. Upon reaching the C.P. the Infantry Captain with field glasses spotted German armor and made radio contact with Sgt. Jones who was stationed nearest the curve and could not see the German tanks. I told him they were entering the curve and just coming into his line of fire so he immediately fired his gun. The first AP shell ricocheted off the front of the Tiger tank. He said, "Did you see that?" I said "Yes" when all of a sudden the German tank, after backing up a little ways, started firing his big gun in a wild manner. After a few minutes he proceeded again to come forward. I warned Jones and the same thing happened as he bounced another shell off the front of that tank. The same sequence was followed as the first time and then on the fourth try the shell found the track. With one track intact the German tank backed up; but soon [sic] the tank (drove into) a roadside ditch. The tank was abandoned and the (German) column retreated to La Glieze. Later a 90mm AA Gun was brought to the hillside on the east and it set the Tiger tank ablaze.[46]

When sentries near Roanne spotted German tanks emerging from the woods bordering La Glieze they began using their 57 mm antitank gun to fire on the nearest Mark V Panther. In the exchange that followed, the antitank gun and 3 A Company tanks managed to disable a Mark V Panther. In the course of the firefight three additional German tanks began moving in the direction of the Shermans. Able Company tanks deployed into defensive positions and held their fire, waiting for the German tanks to close to an effective range for their short-barreled 75s. At that moment the Germans were still too distant, but the Americans were not.

The platoon leader and his gunner dismounted from their tank, thinking to use a few precious moments to look over the terrain. Suddenly an 88 mm shell, fired from one of the approaching German Tiger tanks, tore through the applique armor welded over the sponson. The Sherman tank immediately burst into flames, engulfing the three crew members still inside. The hit by the Mark VI was estimated at approximately 2,000 yards.[47] The German tanks continued to close until A Company's 2d Platoon knocked out one of the advancing Tigers.

On the morning of the 20th the enemy still held part of Stavelot. That same day, Baker Company's 3d Platoon tanks were exploring a street when they unexpectedly encountered a Tiger tank at a range of 50 yards. An accompanying friendly tank destroyer quickly fired one round which bounced off. Tank B15 fired four rounds in rapid succession, all of which also bounced off. The Sherman immediately fired a smoke shell and backed around a corner to safety. For the rest of the day 3d Platoon tanks played a deadly cat and mouse game in Stavelot's streets and alleys with the huge Mark VI Tiger, but were unable to flank the German tank in the narrow village roadways. Finally, the tankers established a roadblock so that if the Tiger tried to break through it could be taken out with a shot into its vulnerable rear armor.[48]

In summer and winter, crews sat in their tanks when expecting action at a roadblock. Battalion tankers had all but forgotten the pleasant Norman weather, when hatches were left open to let as much heat as possible escape from the sun-baked steel hulls. In December the same sun sent long golden rays to haunt, but never warm, the tanks' frost-covered surfaces. Hatches were open by necessity, and the seated driver and his assistant were continually frozen by the air flowing up and over the sloping steel glacis. The great rear-mounted engines sucked the cold winter air through every opening, whether hatch or crevice. The constant draft made it seem even colder than it actually was inside of the hull. Often there was so much condensation in the tank that when the inside air cooled, icicle-studded frost formed around the insides of the hatchways. Unable to leave the tank, crewmen stomped their feet on the metal floor panels. Some sat with extra cloth and newspaper bulging from the tops of their unlacable boots. Fingers thick with woolen gloves grasped at cigarettes and fumbled at range finders, radio dials, and triggers. Anyone needing to relieve himself used what had become a standard utility—a spent shell casing which was afterwards tossed out the nearest hatch.

Conditions permitting, a guard was posted in the turret while the remaining crew members moved into houses or barns. The men under shelter huddled in groups over fires and stoves, their dirty, damp clothing slowly releasing its smell of moist wool scented with gasoline into air heavy with cigarette smoke.

A forward post surrounded by darkness and gripped in winter's chill can be eerily quiet after the excited activity and noise of battle. The solitary guard was left in the dark accompanied only by the smells of spilled fuel and oil that lingered long after the last warmth had disappeared from the engine compartment. Memories of the afternoon rushed to fill the lonely void of the turret as the departing shaft of sullen winter glare, shaped by the roundness of a hatch opening, was replaced by the dim glow of a dome light.

Besides maintaining a lookout, the man on duty kept the tank and radio batteries charged with a small gas-powered generator nicknamed "Little Joe," located inside the rear compartment of the turret. The quietness of an outpost could be suddenly shattered by the tanker pull starting the generator. The little stuttering engine rattled noisily, and white clouds of exhaust wafted lazily outwards from the tank. The sentry could be assured that angered infantrymen would soon appear, swearing that every Jerry for miles around would be warned off, or brought in by the stink and noise.

At a farmhouse roadblock near Stavelot, Earl Dhanse listened to the German 150 mm *Nebelwerfer* rockets sounding like gusts of wind slicing through the snowstorm. The next rocket attack passed over the farmhouse and hit the barn, setting it afire. The explosions blackened the snow-covered ground surrounding the barn and wounded the GIs collected inside. Dhanse and battalion medic Robert Blasser went to the aid of the men, their pain cleary audible amidst the exploding rockets. The wounded were given first aid and loaded into half-tracks and ambulances. Dhanse returned across the barnyard through a fog that further reduced visibility in the increasing snowstorm. The fog had set in during the rocket attack and when Dhanse rejoined his crew in their tank, hatches were kept open because frosted periscopes were of no use. The crewmen were confined to their shortbacked seats the entire night; at daylight they returned stiff with cold to the farmhouse.[49]

December 21 the Assault Gun Platoon pulled out of the front line for a long day of artillery missions. The gun crews ran out of ammo three times and were resupplied by a nearby artillery unit. The day's work accounted for 2 tanks, 3 half-tracks burned or disabled, and 1 mortar battery and ammo dump destroyed. One additional mission was fired on enemy troops advancing in American vehicles.[50] The following day, the assault guns joined with the battalion's Mortar Platoon as they turned back an assault by a group of Tiger tanks and mechanized infantry advancing on Roanne.[51]

When rapid firing the 105 mm gun, the tank confines became a nearly insufferable container of noise, heat, fumes, and activity. Each shell sent an ear-shattering blast reverberating through the air of the tiny compartment. The breach mechanism quickly ejected the shell casing, and as the white whorls of breach gases rushed to escape their chamber, another round was shoved into place and fired. After five minutes of continuous firing, gases from burnt explosives filled the hull, stinging the eyes and burning the lungs of crewmen competing with their neighbors for air. The passive hull-mounted air vents were inefficient and did little to alleviate the thickening stink of cordite. The fan of the great rear-mounted engine provided some aeration, but even this was of little help and crewmen often passed out in the fumes.[52]

Baker Company tankers stationed in Stavelot began their mornings by blowing away the machine gun nests set up during the night in the homes and businesses opposite their positions. This was always followed by continued street fighting. During these engagements white phosphorous was used to burn buildings containing stubborn enemy strongpoints. The burning phosphorous added a garlic-like odor to the smell of discharged weapons already suspended in the dense, cold winter air.

On December 21 the silent snowfall seemed ill-matched with the ear-splitting noises of the house to house fighting. Towards the afternoon the last of the enemy was pushed out of the village and across the Ambleve River. After evening darkness obscured his gunner's vision Harry Hansen fired white phosphorous into the buildings across the Ambleve. The resulting flames lit up the water, and the tankers fired on stragglers crossing under cover of darkness. All night the town received direct fire, heavy mortar, and *Nebelwerfer* rocket fire from the far side of the river. Also during the night, after moving into the former German positions in Stavelot, it was discovered that at least 20 civilian men, women, and children of the village had been murdered.[53]

The presence of the Americans encouraged the townspeople to emerge from their cellars. Soon they were circulating around Joe Couri's tank.

On this particular day, I observed an elderly man with a little covered wagon. He was pulling it and going into a garage directly across from my tank. He had made several trips down the street and when he came back the next time he stopped at my tank. Since I could not speak Belgian, he pulled the cover from the wagon. I have never forgotten the sight of the two children's bodies. There they were, frozen with the older child's arms around the other as they were shot by the SS troops. They were still frozen in that position.[54]

Widespread atrocities were committed against civilians and soldiers during the Bulge offensive. Shortly after the push for Liege began, German SS overran the village of Parfondruy. Civilians from some of the homes were herded into a barn and shot. Twenty-three-month-old Monique Thonon was wounded in the legs as she was being held in the arms of her pregnant mother. A neighbor searched the barn the next day after the SS had left, and discovered the child covered by her mother's body, alive, but partially frozen. The little girl was brought to American soldiers of the 117th Regiment, 30th Infantry Division and taken to the hospital at Verviers. Later that same day the SS returned and burned the barn containing the villagers.[55]

Joe Couri's new defensive position allowed a view of the far bank of the Ambleve River but not the source of the occasional German shells exploding nearby. Direct fire from across the Ambleve River posed a tremendous danger to all the tankers. Direct fire could be from a tank or an antitank weapon ranging in size from 37 mm to 88 mm. A crew of six operating the latter were capable of firing 8 rounds a minute. Designed as an antiaircraft gun it was a particularly frightful weapon when turned on tanks. The tanker under direct fire was in a grey area of possible responses. Direct fire indicated your tank was so close to the enemy's position that a wall, or vehicle, or your own tank took the hit before the sound of the enemy gun was heard. In such cases survivors paid less attention to the object that had been hit, than to ordering quick evasive action. All one could do was pull over into a side street, alongside a barn or house and anxiously wait while eyes sought a movement, or ears perhaps detected the kumpf-like sound of the next round. The crew was on notice of the danger and searched to identify probable locations of the gun. Telltale movements or a subsequent shot brought the 75 to bear on its intended target. Once an adversary was identified, hurried fire orders sent the tank lurching backwards. With the exit of each round, eyes pushed against scopes and binoculars searching for results. Below the turret, the driver pressed his face against his periscope, waiting for the order to move. The danger could be over or the scenario might continue until some unseen and unheard shell exploded through the thin layer of sandbags and steel, filling the interior with fire and shrapnel.

On one such occasion Sergeant Alvin Tisland dismounted from his tank and instinctively ducked at what he thought was a blast from his tank's main gun, accidently triggered by his gunner. Seconds later it was discovered that a nearby German tank had fired an 88 mm shell through Tisland's turret from back to front.

After taking the life of the gunner, the shell exited the gun mantlet, and its sound was momentarily mistaken for the blast of the 75.[56]

On December 24, A Company tankers shot down a German FW-190. Nearby, two Third Armored Division task forces attacked and took La Glieze from a token German force. It had been largely deserted the previous day by Colonel Peiper's men. 3d Armor's action conducted with the 30th Division's 2d Battalion 119th Infantry Regiment liberated 200 men of their regiment taken prisoner in the fighting at Stoumont. Also captured were 200 Germans, 30 tanks (mostly Panther Mark Vs and Tiger Mark VIs), 70 half-tracks, 1 150 mm Assault gun, 1 75 mm Assault Gun, 4 120 mm mortars and other assorted vehicles.[57] On Christmas day a maintenance group representing the battalion visited a field near La Glieze. Of particular interest were the abandoned Mark V and Mark VI tanks. Widespread hopes that they could be converted to battalion use were given up due to maintenance problems.[58] The battalion's desire for a tank equivalent to that of their adversary was shelved indefinitely.

When Anny Maertins de Noordhout learned that American soldiers were living upstairs in their house, she had asked if any of them were from Minnesota. Repeatedly cautioned about providing personal information to civilians, the Americans didn't answer. But later one of the men told Anny that Sergeant Howard Froberg was from Minnesota. Anny and Howard soon discovered that she was a friend of some girls he had known back home, daughters of his father's employer. That night the children, their families, and the men from tank B16 gathered in the basement of the house and sang "Silent Night, Holy Night" around a pine branch decorated with a lone candle.[59]

On Christmas day, Tom Snyder, with Able Company's 1st Platoon went on a mission to verify reports of enemy paratroopers. The reports proved to be untrue. Upon returning, Snyder slowed his tank to talk to a group of soldiers who made it known that a destroyed nearby building had a large wine cellar. When the tank became "missed," Snyder radioed that they were having problems with fouled plugs and would soon rejoin the platoon. Snyder drove to the shell-wrecked building, attached a large trunk to the rear engine deck and filled it with wine. Unsatisfied with the amount of wine held by the trunk, the crew jettisoned the unused rounds stored in the turret and replaced them with additional dark-green bottles.

Metal kits jangling in hand, the long shuffling line of A Company men awaited dinner behind the open-backed mess trucks. Snyder's tank clattered noisily past the disinterested line of waiting men, turned sharply at the front of the mess trucks and stopped. Inside the turret fragile glass bottles rattled noisely in the metal ammo racks. Snyder stood on the engine deck, reached into the trunk and began handing down a bottle to each man receiving dinner. The platoon leader's gruff remark of "Fouled plugs—uh?" couldn't change the fact that with each bottle distributed the crew were hailed as heroes of the day.[60]

On December 30 the battalion prepared to say farewell to 1944 and six months of combat. An unnecessary indignity was added to the year's bitter memories when "friendly" aircraft bombed the battalion's headquarter personnel stationed at Xhoffraix.[61] The distinction between allied or enemy aircraft was a quick affair for seasoned combat veterans whose turret-mounted .50 caliber machine guns were effective antiaircraft weapons. This was never better demonstrated than early one January morning when battalion tanks were visited by raiding enemy fighters flying above the tree tops in the sub-zero temperatures. Baker Company tanks opened fire with their turret-mounted machine guns, and four planes were shot down.[62] When friendly aircraft attacked the battalion's positions, the men held their fire despite the absence of a reciprocal gesture.

Wayne Robinson was a professional journalist in civilian life and joined the battalion's Headquarters Company during the Siegfried Line Campaign. Robinson was chosen from a replacement depot to write the battalion's battlefield history from Colonel Duncan's detailed, daily field notes. Robinson had just set up writing quarters in a bombed grocery in Julich, Germany, when the move into the Bulge was undertaken. Several days after arriving in Malmedy, Robinson made a frightening discovery:

> . . . when things had more or less settled down out-side Eupen and Malmedy, I had a chance to resume "writ-ing" the Battalion history from the Colonel's notes— . . . AND FOUND I DIDNT HAVE THEM! I knew then exactly where they were—on a shelf where I had moved aside the Kraut Jello boxes to make room. There were all those 30th Division papers stamped TOP SECRET which the Colonel had turned over to me. I had visions of a MP jeep driving up looking for Wayne Robinson where I would be summarily courtmartialed and shot!
>
> Fortunately, I had plenty of maps and duplicate pa-pers from S-3 Sgt. Davis so I could fill in all the lost "gaps" again without the Colonel's coordinates and militareze. I wasn't worried about the Germans finding all those "Top Secret" papers—I was worried about Our Side finding them![63]

In its bid for Liege the 1st SS Panzer Division failed to breach the American line at Stavelot and Malmedy. But Von Rundstedt's offensive had pushed to within five miles of the Meuse River and had disrupted Allied plans farther north for crossing the Roer. The rapid American motorization and the containment of German armor paid off. In January, the Americans would go on the offensive.

On January 2, the battalion received M4A1 medium tanks equipped with 76 mm guns. Requested by Colonel Duncan during the hedgerow battles, these tanks were the first for the battalion and were given to Charlie Company's 1st Platoon.[64]

The American offensive began the following day with an attempt by First Army to cut the Germans' three main supply roads leading into the Bulge. Joseph Couri's experiences were typical of the battalion's January frontline action.

January 13th on a bitter cold morning we jumped off. My platoon was attached to the 119th Infantry and we were on the extreme right of the Division. We had moved on the road to Bellevaux, which was mined, disabling a couple of tanks. We took to the deep snowy fields, but mines were there too. There was a fire break in some tall pine trees and, along with the Infantry Company, we decided to go through. A fire fight developed there and the Germans fled, but not all made it.

As we proceeded, my tank bogged down in a low spot as we were nearing the end of the fire break. About this time the German artillery shells started coming our way but going over us. The infantry and my platoon were given orders to log the path in front of my tank. All were put to work getting tree limbs. But the German artillery was getting closer all the time. Finally, they zeroed in on us just as we were getting the tanks out of the forest. The tree bursts hit some infantry men, and I lost one man of my platoon to shrapnel.

From there we made it over the main road to the high ground overlooking Bellevaux where we spent the first night out. This was by far the coldest night that I experienced in the war. After going through the forest with the turret open and the snow tumbling down from the trees on me I was completely wet. The tank had snow in it too. It was what you call a Frigidaire and we were going to try and sleep in it. We were better off than the infantry for it was impossible for a man to dig a fox hole in the frozen ground. They asked if they could bed down for the night under our tanks and they did.

I can say there was not much sleeping that night. The shelling of both sides was continuous throughout the night. We were alerted for a possible counterattack that did not happen. The *Nebelwerfer* rockets (Screaming Meemies) came at us all night long.

January 14th we moved out early to the river bank. Then we turned east to take Bellevaux. Opposition was mostly from artillery, mortars, and rockets. From there we moved out to capture a small nearby village. I dismounted from my tank to meet with the infantry Captain down the road to discuss our next mission. As I was walking on this road I heard the sound of airplanes coming from the north. Looking up, I identified them as our B-26 bombers, a couple of squadrons or more. Just as I was almost to the C.P. I heard this screeching sound of the bombs. Looking up, I knew they were meant for us. With only a few seconds to react I threw myself into a shallow ditch along the roadside. The bombs came down shaking the earth on detonation and boulders of dirt were thrown in the air. That trail of bombs crossed right over me and across the field to another road where the sergeant working with me from the 823d Tank Destroyer unit was killed while he was walking on the road to the C.P.

The house with the C.P. was very fortunate for a bomb exploded next to the foundation throwing all the dirt away from the house exposing a basement wall which was not affected by the blast. Just a matter of a couple of yards saved the lives of all the soldiers in it.[65]

Now within sight of Saint-Vith the 30th Division and 743d tanks increased its pressure on the German troops busied with pulling out everything salvageable from the Saint-Vith salient. The roads were strewn with German tanks, trucks, cars, even horse-drawn sleighs abandoned by the retreating German columns.[66]

Some restrictions always slowed a quick advance. The drive on Saint-Vith was afflicted by bad weather, rough terrain backed up by determined *Panzerfaust* teams, artillery, direct-fire weapons and heavily mined roads. To help in the battle against the ice and snow, the battalion's Service Company welded cleats onto the tank tracks to improve traction. The test using a tank to push a dozer tank through the deep snow was less successful.

No amount of ingenuity could alleviate the recurrent problem posed by mines. From the outset, mines plagued the offensive against Saint-Vith. Over two days, between January 13 and January 15, fifteen tanks were lost to mines.

Concerned about mines, Sergeant Cock Perry Kelly stood in the turret and swore again at his driver to keep the tank, crawling along in low gear, in the mine-free ruts made in the snow by the passage of previous vehicles. Any slight incline or uneven surface sent the tank slipping sideways.

The "thunk" on the outside of the hull brought more swearing from Cock as he turned his head and was momentarily stunned by the unexpected appearance of a soldier with snow frozen in his hair. The tank tracks had passed over the feet of the hidden figure. The weight of the tank jerked the dead soldier from underneath his snowy shroud and now rudely held him in a position of attention.[67]

The dead were less numerous than mines, but of equal concern in the American zone that had been overrun at the outset of the German offensive the month before. Ashley Camp had just climbed down from his tank and seated himself on a snowbank to eat when several men arrived in a jeep and asked him to move. Camp watched as the men used shovels to remove the snow and extract several bodies of servicemen concealed underneath the spot where he had been eating.[68]

While battling towards Saint-Vith three days were needed to dislodge the German 1st Battalion, 9th Parachute Regiment defending Thirimont and a hill near Hauts-Sarts that overlooks the Thirimont-Malmedy-Saint-Vith road. After Thirimont was taken, it had to be defended against repeated counterattacks by the same group until the battalion's light tanks helped take and secure the nearby hill on January 15.[69] Three more days of fighting under sleet and snow and the roadblocks defending Recht were overcome and the town taken.

On January 20, Able Company moved out of Pont with the 119th Infantry Regiment. En route the tanks destroyed 6 antitank guns and numerous machine gun emplacements before arriving at Schlommofurth and Oberts Crombach. In nearby action, Baker Company's 1st Platoon attacked swiftly over roads freshly swept of mines and battled their way to Neder Emmels where they were halted by self-propelled guns, artillery, rockets, and small arms. The drive was parralleled by 2d and 3d Platoons of Charlie Company battling towards Sart-Lez-Saint-Vith. The temporary absence of big German battle tanks was more than made up for by direct fire from artillery as for example when Harlan Whitcomb maneuvered his tank through an underpass while pushing toward Saint-Vith.

> . . . as we came out the other side we were struck by an artillery shell on the turret outside of where I was sitting. The Tank Commander was standing behind me, when I turned around to see what happened, his face was a mass

of blood, he just slid to the floor of the turret behind me. He never knew what hit him.[70]

The next day A Company tankers cleaned up German stragglers and C Company remounted its attack on Sart-Lez-Saint-Vith.[71] The struggle raged over five hours. By the end tank C10 had been hit by direct fire, exploded and burned. But two platoons of Charlie Company tanks had accounted for 4 horsedrawn wagons, a half-track, one Mark IV and 150 prisoners. As 1st and 2d Platoons consolidated their positions, 3d Platoon with the 1st Battalion 117th Infantry attacked through their line, knocking out two more Mark IVs and a horse-drawn ammo wagon.[72]

Further advances were made on the 22d but at an ever greater price. The Assault Gun Platoon fired on Saint-Vith, while Able Company tanks attacked and occupied Hinderhausen and Kapelle. Saint-Vith straddled the junction point of several roads used by the Germans for the transferal of men and supplies to the northern part of the Bulge. Consequently, as the Americans pushed closer, heavy artillery, mortar fire, and direct antitank fire stiffened the German resistance. Sandbagging paid off again when an A Company tank took 4 direct hits that disabled the tank but did not penetrate the hull. At the same time an accompanying tank found a mine. Tom Snyder, the tank's commander and the company's Christmas hero, was seriously wounded.[73] The crewmen evacuated their tanks and headed for the cover of a nearby house. The men were running under heavy incoming artillery when a round exploded in the middle of the group, injuring five more and killing two.

Baker Company's 1st Platoon, in position with the 1st Battalion 120th Infantry Regiment, radioed the battalion's assault guns when they spotted what appeared to be an attempt by the Germans to withdraw some artillery. But suddenly, the Germans counterattacked with three Mark IVs and 100 infantry. The assault gun crews hastily began firing through the woods in the direction of the oncoming attack while two tanks revved their engines to give the impression of an attack from the west. At the same time 1st Platoon's three remaining tanks drove around to the east and attacked the enemy's flank.

The three attacking tanks surprised the column and destroyed one Mark IV at only 150 yards after which the other two withdrew. Because the German infantry were deprived of their armored support the three tanks deployed in line and opened up with HE and machine guns completely breaking up the attack. Only eight doughs had supported 1st Platoon's 3 tanks during the flanking maneuver.[74] This was the last German counterattack of the Bulge. The next day battalion tankers entered Sart-Lez-Saint-Vith so quickly they literally caught the enemy at breakfast.[75]

Limited enemy resistance continued unabated for several more days. To assist the line company Shermans, the Assault Gun Platoon moved back into the front line. Shortly after getting into position they were strafed by a British Spitfire that sent the crewmen outside their tanks scrambling for cover.[76]

Nearby, Captain Joel Matteson of Able Company led 1st and 3d Platoons on an early dawn attack to Krombach while 2d Platoon pushed their way into Weisten. But the hot spot of the day centered on B Company's 3d Platoon attacking Orr Emmels and Neder Emmels with the 120th Infantry Regiment.

Lieutenant Hansen, commanding tank B15, led the infantry attack into Orr Emmels. The group used HE to destroy strongpoints located in the houses and took 80 prisoners. Tank B17 advanced deeper into town and set a Mark IV self-propelled gun on fire with 8 quick-fired rounds from 400 yards. On a nearby side street tank B-16 spotted a second Mark IV self-propelled gun and removed it from action. Shortly thereafter, Hansen spotted yet another Mark IV from his turret and silenced it with 3 rounds of AP and 1 round of HE. Seconds later B16 called target on a fourth Mark IV and put 4 AP rounds into it.

Incredibly enough not everyone was paying attention. The three tanks arrived at the other edge of town and captured 4 Mark IV self-propelled guns and their crews in the barns where they had pulled their vehicles for camouflage. On the way to Neder Emmels with the 120th Infantry's 2d Battalion, another 183 prisoners were captured without a shot being fired by either tanks or doughs.[77]

The 743d and the 30th Infantry Division battled to within three miles of Saint-Vith before the 7th Armored Division attacked through their positions. To the chagrin of battalion tankers and infantrymen alike, photos appeared in newspapers everywhere depicting the entrance to Saint-Vith with a sign stating "Welcome to Saint-Vith Courtesy of the 7th Armored Division."

By January 24 Von Rundstedt's Bulge had collapsed. Saint-Vith was occupied by the Allies, and the Germans had again withdrawn behind the West Wall. The battalion held its positions until the 28th when the tankers moved through a snowstorm to the battered villages of Hebronval and Ottre for rest and resupply in division reserve. The next day Dog Company received new M-24 light tanks armed with 75 mm guns. To prevent confusion among the infantry the new models were prudently shown off to nearby soldiers.

The push to the Roer River had begun on the banks of the Wurm. Interrupted by nearly two months of combat in the Ardennes the battalion could once again turn its attention east.

V

Battles on the Plain of Cologne

TO TAKE THESE TOWNS WITH A MINIMUM NUMBER OF CASUALTIES TO AMERI-
CAN TROOPS WHO WOULD HAVE TO CROSS OVER FLAT OPEN GROUND TO GET
TO THE HOUSES, IT WAS DECIDED TO USE NIGHT ATTACKS.

Colonel Duncan[1]

ADVANCING AT NIGHT WAS DANGEROUS, BUT NOT AS MUCH AS IN DAYTIME.

Ashley Camp, B Company

FEBRUARY brought the first hints of spring and the battalion's
last major battle of the winter campaign. An Allied victory appeared
to be close but the end was not yet apparent—at least not to the
front line tanker and Old Hickory infantrymen.

In division reserve at Hebronval and Ottre the battalion once
again busied itself with the maintenance and sandbagging of its
tanks.

Light but steady rains accelerated the spring thaw, and in the
warming weather, fields, roads, and mines reappeared from
underneath their dirty blankets of snow. The battalion defused
unexploded shells revealed lying about their positions, and souvenir
fever was tempered by the recovery of numerous German small
arms and equipment strewn everywhere about the area.[2]

A nonfraternization film entitled "Your Job in Germany," shown
in a Hebronval café, fueled rumors of a return to the Roer. The rumors
became fact on the afternoon of February 2 when orders were issued
requiring radio silence and the removal or covering of all 743d
markings on tanks and uniforms. That same evening overlay maps
were distributed showing the route of march back into Germany.

The move and all associated information was top secret, for it consisted of shifting the 743d attached to the 30th Infantry Division from XVIII Corps, First Army to XIX Corps, Ninth Army.[3]

Rain-charged grey clouds concealed the early morning departure north. Upon the battalion's arrival, civilians were kept out of the bivouac areas and camouflage was constantly checked and rechecked to help maintain secrecy. While awaiting the next stage of the move the whitewash that had served as winter camouflage was scrubbed off the tanks, and the sandbagging mixture was improved with the addition of cement. For the first time six men received 30-day stateside furloughs.

On February 8, a second march was undertaken using the cover of darkness and rain. The battalion reentered Germany via Aachen, and arrived in the zone of the Ninth Army early the following day. The new bivouac was located near the Reichsautobahn leading to Cologne.

> Most of the buildings in the small town just east of Eschweiler stood in ruins, scarcely habitable. War had seemed to throw the insides of these houses out. The streets were strewn with broken furniture, bits of stoves and kitchen ranges, [and] masses of wet unsightly bedding. To camouflage a tank it was merely necessary to pull part of a former dwelling over it, perhaps tossing a part of a kitchen table on the turret to complete the effect.[4]

The battalion's new positions were situated on the Roer River Plain between Linnich in the north and Dueren in the south, within a few miles of the battalion's December location. The Roer River Plain extends from the German frontier with Holland and Belgium, east towards the Rhine and is part of a larger stretch of mountainless territory which includes the Plain of Cologne located between the Roer and Rhine Rivers. The plains were tank country and the agricultural and industrial communities were a welcome break from the forested terrain of the Ardennes.

The 743d's arrival was followed by a two-week waiting period during which methodical but rapid preparations were made for Operation Grenade—the attack across the Roer River. The men's optimism, however, was discouraged not only by the contrary efforts of the Germans but also by rain and melting snow.

North of First Army's planned crossing sites were three dams holding back tons of water that could be released upon the attacking armies. On February 10, on the eve of the Roer River attack, the Germans destroyed the discharge valves, allowing the slow regular release of the dam waters. The water poured forth for twelve days, swelling the river's breadth from 50 to 300 feet in some areas and increasing its flow to more than 10 mph as the river reached flood level.[5] The German action was designed to provoke delays, not a rapid inundation; and it succeeded.

Postponement of Operation Grenade allowed training, vehicle maintenance, and the improvement of daily living conditions to continue. The delivery of four new Sherman M4A3E2s sporting 76 mm main guns made a welcome addition to the battalion's firepower.[6] Field improvements to the new tanks began immediately, from sandbagging to the welding of ammo-ready racks inside the turrets.[7]

The camouflage discipline, that had been in effect since the battalion's departure from the Ardennes, was continually reinforced. Some vehicles were even moved into vacant buildings. "Old timers" received three-day passes to Paris or to a rest area at Valkenberg, Holland, and movies were shown. As the rainy weather continued, men studied and restudied aerial photos of the attack terrain. Also in preparation for the coming battle the Assault Gun Platoon test-fired its guns with ordnance personnel. The target was the center of Hambach, 11,000 yards away in enemy territory.

Eighty-three returning 743d veterans and new men drawn from replacement depots helped the battalion's line companies reach battle readiness.

On the 19th of February the anxiety of anticipated combat was heightened when it was announced that the flood waters were receding. Platoon leaders made final checks of vehicles and radio equipment, and the Articles of War were read to the men.[8] The elaborate precautions to maintain secrecy during the transfer north from the Ardennes would soon pay off.[9] In the final days before the attack the German Luftwaffe made repeated airstrikes with small numbers of aircraft. Included in the sorties were jet engine fighters, the first thus far encountered and a sharp contrast to German, earthbound, horse-drawn artillery.[10]

Four days later 25 miles of the Roer River exploded when one of the largest artillery barrages was fired on the western front of World War II. Behind the 8,000 yard line where the 743d and the 30th Infantry Division waited, one gun was firing for every 32 yards of enemy river frontage.[11]

From the American side of the river it was an almost unparalleled display—the glare of shells to the east as far as the eye could see to right and left across that flat coun-tryside, while the belch of cannons to the rear broke win-dows and shook great slabs of plaster loose.[12]

A bank of artificial fog 2,000 yards across, 3 to 4 miles long and 2,200 feet high screened the river crossings.[13]

The 743d was to cross the Roer River and assist Old Hickory's attack north along a narrow corridor through the Hambach Forest towards Steinstrass. Steinstrass was the most likely location from which a German counterattack would develop along the main road to Cologne.

Under cover of the final moments of the artillery barrage the infantry crossed the Roer and secured bridgeheads. Meanwhile, engineers started the construction of bridges heavy enough to support the waiting tanks. Wayne Robinson would later write: The bridging operation was an engineer's headache. Actually it wasn't so much a river crossing as it was a crossing of a wide, boggy swamp with a current of six miles an hour.[14]

During the night Able Company drove to Inde where they rendezvoused with their guides. The guides took A Company across the Inden River and north to Shophaven, then east across the Roer.[15] By 5 A.M., the company was in position at Hambach. Shortly thereafter Baker and Charlie Companies passed through A Company positions on their way to Krauthausen and Niederzier. One hundred and fifty yards from Krauthausen German prisoners were helping to construct treadway bridging over the Roer.[16] Elsewhere, westbound German prisoners were already crossing the river on footbridges. C Company used the leapfrog tactic, first tried while battling for the Siegfried Line, to join Baker Company at Niederzier. After their arrival B Company's 3d Platoon fought its way north in the direction of Steinstrass under the supporting fire of Charlie Company.[17]

The tankers' day had started before dawn, and it was coming to a quick end under a somber, late winter sky. Nonetheless, 3d Platoon's confidence in the success of a continued attack on Steinstrass was high due to the six tank destroyers and three British flail tanks reinforcing the group. Shortly after deciding to press on against various sized antitank guns, progress stalled when three of the platoon's tanks were disabled at a mined roadblock. Battalion crewmen and the six infantrymen riding the rear decks chose to abandon the damaged tanks when two Panther Mark Vs moved up for the kill. The remaining two tanks of 3d Platoon began firing on the Panthers, now six hundred yards away, while the British flail tanks tried to clear a path through the minefield. In response, the Panther crews swiftly knocked out the lead British tank at the same time that 20 hits were recorded on the three disabled tanks.[18] Unable to identify their targets in the darkness, the remainder of the force withdrew and dispersed for the night. The next day the mines were removed from around the vehicles, and by midafternoon the roadblock was cleared. Baker Company's 3d Platoon pulled back, and Able Company's 1st Platoon took over.

Many German tanks were equipped with a factory-applied antimagnetic paste called *zimmerit* to reduce the effectiveness of hand-placed magnetic mines. *Zimmerit* coatings gave tanks a rough-patterned finish. But such coatings were ineffective against either Allied or German mines that required weight for ignition. Two nonmetallic German mines sometimes found together at roadblocks were the antipersonnel *Schuh* mine and the antitank *Topf* mine. After the *Topf* mine brought the tank to a halt, crewmen and infantrymen were at risk from the *Schuh* mines. Neither mine was detectable by standard mine detection means. Several other types of mines were also frequently encountered. The long, rectangular *Riegel Mine 43* antitank mine contained nearly nine pounds of explosive. Another antitank mine was the round *Tellermine 42* weighing approximately the same as the *Riegel* mine but needing the weight of a vehicle to set off its 12-pound explosive charge. To deny tank crews their accompanying infantry, *S-mines* might be employed also. *S-mines* consisted of a long-necked cylinder full of ball bearings topped by thin metal prongs that were left exposed above the soil or snow. When the prongs were stepped on, the resulting explosion blew bits of the mine and ball bearings into the air.

Steinstrass had become the proverbial intractable thorn in its ability to draw blood and frustrate. Well-designed minefields channelled the attacking tanks into the sights of waiting German antitank guns and tanks. Another difficulty facing the troops were the German tanks hidden alongside houses in Steinstrass's streets. Consequently, the battalion's Assault Gun Platoon moved east of Hambach and, under the guidance of 743d forward observers, made the houses their targets. After a call for fire was received, several shots were registered on the target house. Then all six 105 mm guns were brought to bear on the single dwelling, sending as many rounds as was necessary to destroy the tank. The Assault Gun crew's concentrated fire was referred to as a Time on Target or TOT. With a TOT all the shells from a number of guns burst simultaneously on the same target. A TOT had a demoralizing effect on the enemy because it arrived without warning and because the simultaneous firing made it difficult for enemy observers to identify the location of the individual guns. On one occasion as many as 120 rounds were fired on a single tank.[19] Following a successful hit, the guns would be sighted onto another house and the action repeated.

While the Assault Gun Platoon made house calls in Steinstrass, A Company's 1st Platoon moved north to the edge of the woods forming a part of the Hambach Forest. Once there, they waited 400 yards west of town until a friendly artillery barrage signalled the moment to attack. Two 1st Platoon tanks, fully loaded with munitions and fuel, emerged from cover and began driving east on the main highway, firing their main guns as they advanced.[20] A few hundred yards down the road direct fire from the southeast tore through the vulnerable side plates of the first tank causing it to flame up. Black smoke squeezed from every opening, roaring into a shapeless dark cloud that concealed the tank. The driver, Bob Anderson, escaped the burning hulk just as the second tank was struck and began burning. German machine gun and small arms fire raked the two tanks as Anderson lunged for the roadside embankment only to find himself in the sights of the Germans' weapons. Pulling himself to his feet, the slight figure of Anderson dashed back across the road seeking the cover of the opposite ditch. When the lead tank was struck, the force of the explosion blew tank commander and platoon leader, 1st Lieutenant Orlyn Folkestad through the open turret hatch. He picked himself up and moved to the second burning tank—now rolling backward—and pulled the stunned assistant driver out of the tank and into the ditch.[21]

The flanking fire virtually stopped the forward momentum of the attack. Without delay, the Germans launched a massive counterattack that was halted by the battalion's Assault Gun and Mortar Platoons.[22] Afterwards battalion medics evacuated five A Company casualties.

With two of 1st Platoon's five tanks burning, the remaining tanks waited while the infantry used the nearby woods to bypass the route. Nonetheless, the German positions in the town proved unrelenting. Seven more hours passed before the tanks entered Steinstrass to set up defensive positions under cover of smoke fired in the last moments of another intensive artillery bombardment. Unable to rout all the German armor in their path, B Company tanks were ultimately forced to withdraw to Niederzier and Julich and from there drove to Steinstrass, reaching the objective shortly after A Company's arrival.

The battalion's assault across the Roer River was the costliest since leaving the Ardennes. Two tanks had been destroyed, three disabled, two crewmen killed, five wounded and two missing in action, all from A and B Companies.[23] Ahead were more open fields dotted with farmsteads and tree-lined roads. Behind the new front line trees blasted into branchless trunks broke the grey skyline. Where the walls of houses still stood their tileless roof timbers looked like broken matchsticks.

In response to the continual need for any improvement of the battlefield coordination and control of tanks and infantry the 743d had acquired the use of an artillery spotter's L-4 observation plane.

During the Roer River attack Major Clarence Benjamin, the battalion's executive officer, had maintained an air-ground liaison from the plane. Benjamin kept one channel of his radio on the Division Artillery frequency and the other channel on the 743d's Headquarter's frequency. This allowed him to contact anyone from division artillery to the battalion commander, company commanders, the battalion's mortar platoon leader, or the battalion's liaison officer at Infantry Division Headquarters. The tank-infantry teams could now count on direct air observation when planning and executing attacks.[24]

After successfully disrupting the Germans' hold on Steinstrass, A Company tanks attacked Lich while B Company tanks held defensive positions in Steinstrass. The leapfrog-like strategy employed by A and B Companies would be given a new twist when executed during night attacks with support from the battalion's assault gun and mortar platoons and the 823d Tank Destroyer Battalion.

Night warfare was something new. From the outset of combat, nighttime for the battalion had been devoted to the consolidation of new positions, the evacuation of wounded, rest and resupply. The primary difficulty during night combat in a tank was that all of the tools normally used during daylight hours were now to be used in near darkness. Although some experimentation with infrared sights was already under way at the army's proving ground at Aberdeen, it would be years before night vision equipment arrived on the battlefield.[25] Night operations were preceded by intensive and thorough study of aerial photographs melded with a confidence in your instincts and those of others with extensive battle experience. But even these advantages would not reveal the bomb craters or minefields hidden in the dark.

Previously only one night attack had been attempted by the battalion. During the Siegfried Line Campaign, 30th Division infantry became pinned down outside of Altdorf. Two thousand yards of flat fields separated the town from the troops and tanks. Baker Company's commander led a predawn attack on foot that succeeded not only in taking the town without accident, but also in forcing seven German tanks to retreat across the Roer River, leaving one tank abandoned inside town.[26]

Under the cool moonlit sky of February 26, A and C Company tanks and infantry attacked the 9th and 11th Panzer Divisions defending Oberembt.[27] Bad luck plagued the outset of the attack. Only thirty minutes after departing, two tanks tipped into deep bomb craters in what turned out to be a minefield. A T-2 and two additional tanks responded to the call for assistance. During the confusion, two enemy tanks moved in and placed everyone under fire. Just after the first tank was pulled out of the bomb crater it was struck and began burning. Within minutes the T-2 and another tank were hit and immediately flamed up. The burning tanks brightly illuminated the remaining men and vehicles. After a fourth tank was hit, the enemy armor withdrew.

Charlie Company tanks came under direct fire again outside Oberembt. Although one tank was hit and exploded into flames, only two crew members received slight burns. After battering their way into Oberembt, A Company tankers were surprised to discover two abandoned enemy tanks, engines idling. Whenever encountering what appeared to be an operable tank, the crews blasted it with a round of HE to see "if anyone was home." During the battle, C Company's lead tank also knocked out a 380 mm rocket firing *Sturmtiger*, a self-propelled howitzer mounted on a Mark VI chassis.[28] The assault group secured the town within two hours and set up defensive positions.

The night's advance route was clearly indicated by the furiously hot, dark bottomed pyres where the battalion's tanks sat burning. Under a lightening sky a rising early morning breeze sometimes distorted the dark columns of smoke, and at other times heavier gusts carried the odors of the burning tanks to ground then up into the tree tops. For the rest of the day the three line companies held their new positions, refueled and maintenanced while awaiting nightfall.

Just before midnight on February 26, A Company prepared to leave Oberembt and attack Putz. Prior to A Company's attack B and C Companies were to jointly attack Kirch. Charlie Company would then hold the town while Baker attacked through the new position towards Troisdorf. With the previous night's minefield incident firmly in everyone's memory, a squadron of British flail tanks was assigned to operate with B Company during the attack.[29] The British firepower was a welcome addition to the company's eleven tanks, that included two borrowed from Headquarters for the evening.[30]

At a prearranged time, B Company tankers halted at their assembly area to call for and await an artillery concentration on Kirch, about 900 to 1000 yards distant. Like the previous night, the plan called for using an artillery bombardment so that the resulting fires would illuminate the target in the darkness. The After Action Reports of that night record what happened next.

While waiting, tank movement was noticed to the left. No one but enemy was known to be in that direction so the lead tank fired at the movement. The warning was issued to the rest of the column which immediately deployed and proceeded to knock out 4 tanks.[31]

It wasn't until some moments later that the four tanks were identified as British. Their leader had lost his way and had veered to the left of the planned advance. They were searching for their missed route when they encountered the waiting B Company tanks.[32] Infantry medics were the first to provide aid to the three most serious cases after which the company's medical detachment evacuated the remaining twelve men. The column then reassumed its attack on Kirch.

Nearby, Able Company had commenced its attack on Putz. Enemy small arms fire kept the infantry pinned down until the tanks could deploy and suppress the fire with their own machine guns. The doughs advanced to defensive positions at the edge of town under the tankers' steady stream of fire. Shortly after, the tanks and troops broke into the streets. The end of the gunfire in Putz coincided with an expanding band of light along the horizon.

The return of daylight combat brought a return of high casualties. Midmorning four B Company tanks attacked Hohenholz in an attempt to protect the flanks of the force assigned to take Königshafen. The tracks of the advancing tanks bit deep into the wet soil, spitting forth clumps of dark colored mud. Fifty yards from the objective they halted briefly to allow the infantry to dismount from the rear decks when direct fire hit the lead tank and set it aflame. The platoon's remaining tanks knocked out the attacking Mark V while it was seeking to reposition itself. It was later discovered that four additional Panthers were working the same area between Hohenholz and Königshafen. Coy and secretive, the Panther crews allowed two other Shermans to advance within 200 yards before hitting and burning the B Company tanks.[33]

To reach Königshafen two platoons of tanks, one each from B and C Company, attacked through Kirchherten where two more tanks were lost to direct fire. Once inside Königshafen two Panthers were knocked out, but not before four additional 743d tanks were ablaze.

The tankers divided up among the infantry. One group concentrated on cleaning up the south end of town while the remainder cleared the north. Another fourteen hours of fighting was necessary before Königshafen was taken. The daytime action cost the battalion nine tanks. Still further losses would be inflicted on B Company the following day.

Early the next morning an enemy tank approached Königshafen. The tank crew standing sentry fired two rounds in quick succession and watched as both shots bounced off the Mark

V's frontal plate. The Panther crew fired. The single round penetrated the sandbags and the armor of the glacis before setting fire to the vehicle; two crewmembers were killed outright, three wounded.

Cock Kelly poked through the torn and tattered buildings near his tank and discovered that he was parked beside a dye works. Throughout the skeleton of the building were containers and vats of very color imaginable. Fervent of his Irish heritage, the temptation was too great. Cock scooped up several cans of green powder, returned to his tank and started painting the sandbagging a bright beautiful green. The excitement was shortlived. Movement over the bags tinted hands and clothing the same bright green, and worse still, under even the lightest of rains a green stain dripped through hatches and crevices.[34]

The crossing of the Roer River and the bold and innovative night tactics experimented with around Cologne had substantially reduced the risks of attacking in full daylight across open stretches of ground. However, as was often the case, combat difficulties were closely associated with inadequate equipment, particularly the lack of mine-clearing tanks.

The 743d's and 30th Division's front line night operations ultimately broke the enemy's resistance along XIX Corps' front. These night attacks also opened the door for the 2d Armored Division to race out over the Cologne Plain towards Düsseldorf and the Ruhr.[35] No further night attacks were undertaken by the battalion for the duration of the war. The battle of Königshafen had cleared the last enemy obstacle on the Plain of Cologne. The battalion now sat on the banks of the Rhine.

VI

On a Street in Magdeburg

THEY HEARD THE ANNOUNCEMENT OF VICTORY AND TOOK IT FOR GRANTED.
THEY ASKED: WHAT NEXT? THEY ASKED: *WHERE* NEXT?[1]

THE battalion never again witnessed a civilian population, like that of Kerkrade, ruthlessly shoved into its path. Still, the human element that would make its appearance in the coming months was no less sorrowful. The strain on the German state resisting the pressures of combined eastern and western fronts frequently showed itself in the weeks ahead. As the cracks in the German military and political structure widened, the variety of human effluence squeezed through the openings became another means of measuring the Reich's dissolution.

Over the next two months the battles participated in by the battalion would contain every danger thus far encountered. But now the nature of battle changed again. The Germans defended fewer positions and attempted to conduct an orderly withdrawal while fighting a rearguard action. Panzer V's capable on an individual basis of holding a platoon or more of Shermans in check were now jealously protected by their crews as if reckless expenditure could not be allowed.

The 743d quietly started March in bivouac at Kirchherten. The respite was brief. During the night of March 1 enemy infantry, supported by seven tanks, attacked from the southwest, cutting the main southwest-northeast supply route of I Company of the 83d Infantry Division located in Kapellen. After surrounding the unit the German force battled its way into the streets. Able Company tanks were alerted the next morning and assigned the task of not only breaking the encirclement but also of retaking the town.[2]

Typical of the engagements of the waning months of the war the tankers met little resistance. After Lieutenant Jenkins knocked out one Mark V the remaining tanks withdrew, all the while returning direct fire. The withdrawal of the enemy tanks from Kapellen was achieved in part, by the 743d's effective use of its new air observation post.

Major Benjamin circled above the battlefield coordinating A Company movements in Kapellen and calling in P47s to attack enemy guns concealed in the nearby forest. On this occasion, Benjamin's light plane narrowly escaped the enemy antiaircraft guns that brought fire onto the craft four separate times during the two and a half hour mission.[3]

The German countryside, especially the forests, resembled a no man's land controlled by wandering bands of German stragglers. The towns occupied by the battalion were centers of quiet and an almost garrison-like lifestyle. When first occupying a town all German males between 16 and 60 were interviewed. All military-active males were evacuated to the rear, even those undergoing medical recuperation in their homes.

It was rare to find a settlement untouched by the destruction wrought by the forward sweep of the front. Therefore, after securing roadblocks and establishing defensive perimeters the primary activity was to clear bomb-scattered trash and gather recoverable furniture for use in habitable dwellings. Replacements attended training programs in map reading, tank gunnery, and medium tank tactics. At the same time Service Company performed much needed maintenance on the tanks and safety was given top priority as the new and old tanks were re-sandbagged. Beginning in March, the battalion's Service Company started welding racks on tank hulls to receive sand-filled mortar ammunition boxes. This new innovation replaced the sandbags that previously had to be tied on.[4] Sometimes the brief occupation of a town was accompanied by the all too rare luxury of hot baths, hot food, hair cuts, and dental care.

In March the battalion was sent back across the Roer to Gangelt, near the Dutch border, for rest and training prior to the Rhine River crossing. A Company led the move beginning at 0800; it ended that afternoon with the arrival of Headquarter and Service Companies.

Evacuated of civilians, Gangelt was a ghost town. The first task as always was the cleaning up of the windowless, shell-torn houses the battalion would occupy. With the trash and litter cleared away, the men set up a theater and barbershop, and hot showers were followed by 14-hour passes to Holland. Crews continued their activities of cleaning, maintenance, and re-sandbagging. Sandtables were constructed for instruction purposes, and a flame thrower school was also established.[5]

While the battalion made Gangelt a habitable place, the surrounding countryside still held its dangers. On March 15 George Preble was driving his jeep down a road when he hit a mine. Preble escaped with eardrum damage and slight wounds to the arm. A wire with a sign warning of mines was hung across the road. But then, while trying to recover Preble's damaged jeep, another battalion member was wounded when his vehicle detonated a second mine.[6]

The battalion crossed the Roer for a third time on March 21 on their way to the lush farming region of Hoog and Kalvershof north of Düsseldorf. In anticipation of the crossing of the Rhine River, the battalion's identity was repainted on all the vehicles. C Company of the 736th Tank Battalion equipped with amphibious Duplex Drive M4s joined the battalion for the assault. With little else to do but wait, the warm spring weather encouraged softball games in the greening pastures. Clothes were washed, letters written and the wandering livestock tended to.[7]

By mid-March the German rearguard had withdrawn across the Rhine River behind hastily erected fieldworks and barriers. The defense of the eastern bank of the Rhine River was given over to a shallow line of regular infantry and Volksgrenadier Divisions. Opposite the Allies' northern section only the 116th Panzer Division and the 15th Panzer Grenadier Division were capable of counterattacking.[8]

Ninth Army was given the task of holding a narrow front line stretching from Düsseldorf to the Lippe River at Wesel. From there they were to cross the Rhine, attack due east and connect with First Army fighting northwards from the Remagen bridgehead. This would complete the encirclement of the Ruhr industrial region.

The evening of the 23d filled the tankers with the same nervous apprehension that always accompanied the wait for battle. The relative quietness of the night was shattered just after midnight when the battalion's Assault Gun Platoon joined other artillery laying down the pre-assault barrage. In an hour and a half of continuous fire the crews manning the battalion's five guns fired 1030 rounds of HE.[9] At 2 A.M., March 24, the attack across the Rhine began from just south of Wesel.

Bright orange ribbons streaking through the early morning darkness marked the ongoing artillery barrage passing over the Duplex Drive (DD) tanks of the 736th. After gaining the eastern banks, the canvas shrouds were lowered and the tanks started fighting inland. The lumbering DD tanks of the 736th's C Company joined the 2d Battalion, 117th Infantry, for an attack on Spellen. Almost immediately the DDs encountered mines. Unable to backtrack, two of the unsandbagged tanks were set afire.

Meanwhile, on the western bank Able and Baker Company tankers moved to their forward assembly areas, drove down the embankments, and boarded Bailey rafts powered by large outboard motors. Various naval groups were transporting the men and equipment necessary to hold the eastern bridgehead in rapid ten-minute trips. Memories of the Roer River crossing came to mind when one of the ferries got out of control and crashed into a pontoon bridge being constructed by engineers. One tank was lost.

The early morning river fog was supplanted by smoke laid around the crossing areas to further conceal the engineers constructing the pontoon bridges. From the air, morning's sharp light revealed the broad expanse of haze-covered river. But the calm outward appearance was underlain by rapid orderly activity. Beneath the constantly renewed smoke cloud, engineers worked feverishly to complete their bridges, and naval craft commanded by seamen traversed back and forth, ferrying soldiers and vehicles to the eastern bank.[10]

At dawn, Major Benjamin went aloft in the battalion's light airplane. Benjamin reported his observations to Division Headquarters using a tank radio installed in the plane. In turn, the battalion was informed by telephone. From his vantage point Benjamin observed that by 8:30 the engineers had placed six pontoon sections, at noon 36 sections, and that by 3:30 the pontoon bridge over the Rhine was complete.[11]

All this time the roar and crash of artillery kept the early morning air vibrating. During the day the battalion's five Assault Guns fired 2021 rounds in addition to those fired during the pre-dawn bombardment. The firing was being done so quickly that the tanks and their supporting half-track crews were unable to prepare ammo quickly enough. Additional men had to be sent up to help prepare shells and dispose of casings.

In an attempt to bypass the stalled tanks of the 736th, 743d A Company tankers and members of the 119th Infantry Regiment attacked and took Friedrichsfeld.

That afternoon, when the engineers had finished the pontoon bridge, priority was given to infantry and artillery traffic while remaining tanks were detained in forward assembly areas. The 743d's Assault Gun Platoon had been ordered to move aross the Rhine to Schanzenberg but was halted by Military Police who took the tanks to be tanks and hence without permission to cross the river at that time. After some technical explanations Sergeant Lindquist convinced the police that his platoon's 105 mm guns were indeed artillery pieces, and the 743d's five assault guns were the first tanks to drive across the pontoon bridge.[12]

The next day the attack continued while the remainder of the battalion moved to the east bank of the Rhine. In front was Able Company with the DD tanks of the 736th. After making contact with their attached infantry they attacked Hunxe where 20 mm and 75 mm antitank guns offered considerable resistance from the woods bordering the town.[13] With the assault on Hunxe under way the Assault Gun Platoon and B, C, and D Companies joined forces in supporting the infantry attacking Dorsten.[14] Plans to carry the fight through to the next town changed when the 116th Panzer Division counterattacked.[15] The Americans' headlong rush was turned into a slow aggressive advance that lasted the rest of the day.

The ability of Panthers' crews to bring a Sherman to task was not yet over. This was aptly demonstrated when two Charlie Company tankers were killed by direct tank fire. A Company tanks continued attacking along the Lippe Canal towards Gahlen where they also came under direct fire. Two of the company's new 76 mm M4s were hit and burned with five men killed and five men MIA. To back up the line company Shermans the battalion's Assault Gun Platoon fired 378 rounds to disrupt enemy armor building for counterattack. At the end of the day, 5 Mark Vs and 5 self-propelled guns defending Gahlen retreated under covering fire.[16]

Aside from the ever-present mines travel on hard-surfaced roads posed few problems, but the spring rains had turned secondary roads into muddy bogs. On the 28th the attack slowed due to the continued, forced use of secondary roads that often amounted to little more than muddy trails. Small logs and straw, when it was available, were used to keep the tanks and vehicles from bogging down in the deeply rutted roadways. When the corduroy roads of logs and straw failed, the battalion's T-2s were kept busy recovering the tanks mired in the muddy ground.

Conditions in the front lines resembled those of February in the Ardennes. Alongside the hard-surfaced main roads graphic evidence of the German retreat was everywhere present. The roads were clogged with numerous horsedrawn wagons, carts, and artillery, some with horses killed in their harnesses.

German forces withdrew deeper into the Reich after four days of hard fighting that held the bridgehead to under twelve miles of penetration. The Rhine defenses, like so many instances before, consisted of a hard crust which, when broken, allowed quick thrusts to the next point of stiffened resistance. With the pressure relieved from the front line the battalion prepared itself for a rapid advance. Proof that the strategy General McNair first initiated was still operating, came after five days of fighting for the bridgehead when the 8th Armored Division passed through the battalion's positions.[17]

On March 31 the possibility of a quick end to the war seemed imminent when maps were distributed showing the entire planned route of the 2d Armored Division with Berlin at the end of the line.[18] April 1, Easter Sunday, brought confirmation of a respite from continuous frontline work. The battalion alongside Old Hickory was to follow the 2d Armored Division, secure its flanks, guard its supply lines, and take care of any resistance that might be bypassed in its plunge toward Berlin.[19] All vehicles were lightened up in anticipation of a quick-paced rearguard action behind the rapidly moving armored divisions. Crews retained only the most essential supplies and equipment so that extra oil and gas could be carried.

The 2d Armored Division initiated its thrust towards Berlin during the first days of April. The battalion's road marches began to resemble those of the previous autumn. The drives were always followed by a quick servicing of the vehicles, a short rest, and then a return to the road early the following morning. Generally, the road marches consisted of 40 to 50 mile drives through the rainy afternoons of early April and sometimes into the darkness of night. With tanks travelling at only 8 to 10 miles per hour the advance would not seem to be a lightning thrust. But to a battalion used to grappling for gains of a little as a half-mile the pace seemed like a marathon.

The columns pressed eastward against a thick flow of foot traffic consisting of recently freed POWs and large numbers of Poles, Russians and other non-German laborers. One evening, when setting up bivouac, a barn was discovered containing 150 Polish and Russian men and women.[20] After arriving at a day's destination the unit could also expect to collect German deserters, many disguised as civilians. Unlike France, Holland, and Belgium, there were no crowds lining the streets. In those towns that had not been evacuated eye contact was often made first with figures half-hidden behind curtained windows.

Roadblocks and defensive positions were established at every bivouac and every temporary stop. At one roadblock PFC John Roncevich was searching through the light but steady rain for figures silhouetted against the distant forest when two soldiers emerged from the woods. Draped in long field coats, the men were walking across the field bordering the woods. When a short burst from the assistant driver's .30 caliber failed to bring a response, another longer burst was fired. To the tank crew's surprise the two soldiers were fourteen-year-olds who had just abandoned their weapons in the forest. Briefly interrogated, one of the lads led crew members back to the arms cache, and then both were sent back for processing as POWs. The seventeen- and eighteen-year-old veterans resumed their lookout reflecting in disbelief on the thought of fourteen-year-old soldiers.[21]

During the day the tankers waved the German soldiers shuffling slowly past their roadblocks on to the rear. At night a wariness born of combat experience required all approaching soldiers to respond to the challenge of "Halt" or "Kamerad." Sporadic exchanges of fire continued through the night, for not everyone approaching a forward post wished to surrender.

2d Armor's plunge beyond the Rhine slowed and then halted at Detmold, Germany's equivalent to America's armor training center at Fort Knox. As 2d Armor's tanks pulled back, the battalion took over and prepared to do what it did best—defeat German strongholds and create a gap through which armored divisions could lunge.

Detmold was situated on a high north-south ridge paralleling the Rhine valley, and it was expected that the taking of it would present a difficult battle. In preparation for the upcoming attack, the battalion's Assault Gun Platoon moved up to join the 230th Field Artillery. On the same gray, rainy day Headquarters Company moved to Verl to be closer to the ridge line.

After moving into the front line, the battalion and Old Hickory infantrymen encountered German patrols and were harassed indirectly by sniper and artillery fire. Over night an enemy patrol penetrated the outer defensive line but it was scattered by grenades and Tommy gun fire from the tank crews. The threat registered by 2d Armor never developed.[22] In preparation for the assault on Detmold B and C Companies and 3d Battalion 120th Infantry first mounted an attack on Hiddesen. Within an hour and a half the town was cleared. One half hour later at 6 P.M. the attack on Detmold began with all three line companies and 1st Battalion of the 120th Infantry Regiment.[23] The 300 soldiers defending Detmold were without supporting mortar, direct or indirect artillery fire, and were expected to hold the town with only small arms and *Panzerfausts*. Faced with the prospect of a bloody onesided battle against a battalion of infantry and two tanks companies the Detmold garrison soon surrendered. In stark contrast to what had been expected only light resistance was met and within an hour 300 prisoners were taken.[24]

The following day Lieutenant Jones of Able Company experienced a similarly spectacular bloodless experience. In mopping up operations with the division infantry near Lemgo, Jones took a tank into a village and was surprised to find a general with 500 soldiers "lined up at attention, guns piled in one part of the courtyard, equipment piled neatly in another."[25]

Nearby at Helpka the light tanks of Dog Company had set up a road block commanding the junction of three roads. Throughout the day and into the night German soldiers walked down the roads to the light tank positions. The men were checked for weapons and sent on to the rear.

At the same time that the medium tanks of A, B, and C Companies continued their guardianship of the 2d Armored Division's flanks, D Company's light tanks scoured the countryside behind the advance. Most of the region's inhabitants had never before seen an American soldier. The light tanks went from village to village, house to house, woods to woods. The numerous prisoners found scattered about were turned over to the 30th Infantry Division.

When a German supply depot was discovered containing a stock of flavored gin referred to as "Jenever Juice," two bottles were distributed to every tanker. The distribution celebrated an end to a successful Rhine crossing.[26]

As the days passed, it quickly became evident that any apparent military and political cohesiveness in the Reich was only a reflection of the past and that the present was much more disorganized and dangerous. Snipers made the roundup even slower and more dangerous in the wooded hills around Dorpe.[27] In areas where the enemy lacked strong organization, resistance sometimes took on a guerilla-like flavor with its accompanying fluidity. For example, on April 8 it was necessary for Able Company to return to Lemgo to clean out a group of soldiers that had moved into the vacuum left after the surrender of the general and his men. On other occasions a lone enemy plane would strafe or drop antipersonnel bombs on the columns of advancing tanks and men.

After crossing the Weser River—the last river before the Elbe and Berlin—ME109s strafed the columns. One plane was brought down by antiaircraft fire.[28] The brief aerial attack hinted that Braunschweig, an important communications center with extensive factories and railroad yards, would be defended. Consequently 2d Armor swept around the city; not through it. However, the German ability and means to resist in the west had changed. When the Braunschweig commander rejected an opportunity to surrender, the battle for the city began April 11 and was over the same day.[29]

Training with the Grant medium tank, Fort Lewis, Washington, 1942.
Photo Orlyn Folkestad

The Sherman Duplex Drive (DD) tank with its canvas sides raised. This is the way the battalion's DD tanks looked as they entered the waters off Omaha beach.
Author's collection, courtesy of Carl Tarlowski

**743d tankers and 30th
Infantry Division infantrymen
near Mortain, August 1944.**
Photo Orlyn Folkestad

**Bringing in prisoners near
Mortain, August 1944.**
Photo Orlyn Folkestad

French civilians serving wine to tankers. Near Domfront, August 1944.
Photo Orlyn Folkestad

German Panther tank knocked out by the 743d, Normandy, August 1944. Note that one of the 743d's T-2 tank recovery vehicles is towing the Panther off the roadway.
Photo Howard Froberg

German Panther tank knocked out by the 743d, Normandy, August 1944. Note that this one received two hits, one to the tracks and another to the thin side armor above the turret race.

Photo Howard Froberg

"Andre," the French Resistance fighter astride the barrel of "Two Time Loser," with Perry "King Cock" Kelly in Tank 14, 743d A Company, 3d Platoon.

Author's collection, courtesy of Charles Brown

Howard Froberg
Photo Orlyn Folkestad

Floyd Jenkins beside a late model 75 mm Sherman M4 with muzzle brake.
Photo Orlyn Folkestad

Henry Schicks preparing a meal on a Coleman stove.
Photo Orlyn Folkestad

Tom Snyder, lower right. Note the heavy sandbagging covering the glacis.
Photo Orlyn Folkestad

Back row left to right: unidentified; Capt. Joel Matteson; Lt. Jones; unidentified; Lt. Jenkins. Front row left to right: Lt. Folkestad; Lt. Mason; Lt. Hastalis; Lt. Couri.

Photo Orlyn Folkestad

Two A Company tanks destroyed outside of Steinstrass, Germany, 1945.

Photo Orlyn Folkestad

German Panther tank knocked out by the 743d.

Photo Don Mason

Battalion halftrack with 50 caliber machine gun mounted on cab.
Collection of author, courtesy Perry Kelly

Road march on the autobahn.

Photo Don Mason

Late model 75 mm Sherman M4A3E2, Spring 1945.

Photo Orlyn Folkestad

Stop at a German airfield, Summer 1945. Note the T-2 tank recovery vehicle at left and three different models of the Sherman M4.

Photo Orlyn Folkestad

A Sherman M4A3E2 with Duckbill extenders on tracks.

Photo Orlyn Folkestad

Sherman M4A3E2 on the right in front of an older Sherman M4 equipped with a long-barreled 75 mm and muzzle brake.

Photo Orlyn Folkestad

Tex Anderson with
Wolf. A Company, 3d
Platoon, mascot.
Photo Orlyn Folkestad

Photo beside glider
mentioned in last
chapter.
Photo Orlyn Folkestad

**German surrendering. As seen
through wheeled vehicle.**
Photo Orlyn Folkestad

**Same individual with Lt. Jones,
and others.**
Photo Orlyn Folkestad

**Same individual with Lt. Jones,
and others.**
Photo Orlyn Folkestad

German railway guns. Harz mountains, 1945.

Photo Don Mason

743d tanks parked in Germany at end of war.

Photo Orlyn Folkestad

The battalion was moving so quickly through the small villages and towns that at night the men slept beside their parked vehicles. As always during the night, crews rotated the watch kept from the turret. At night, weak overhead lights replaced the sunlight highlighting the dust drifting through open hatches. The dim dome lights enhanced the shadowed interiors tainted by the smell of cigarettes, oil, gas and the residual smell of the dirty companions who slept nearby. But now only a replacement would have taken notice.

The long drives continued with infantry riding on the rear decks. The rapid pace was maintained in an attempt to grab bridges before their demolition. But often upon approaching river and stream crossings the sounds of explosions presaged the obvious.[30] Still, the rapid eastward push was catching many uniformed Germans by surprise. On April 12 A Company's 1st Platoon overran an enemy airfield north of Helmstedt capturing various planes and vehicles dispersed in the nearby woods. When one fighter tried lifting off Sergeant Fawcett, a battalion D-Day veteran, shot it down with his turret-mounted 50 cal. machine gun.[31]

When battalion tankers drove into one side of a town they often observed their enemy moving out the other. The same day the airfield was captured, Dog Company light tanks were attacking the nearby town of Cremlingen. When tank D12 called for infantry help, and none appeared, the platoon leader broke the rules of tank-infantry coordination and attacked. The light tanks entered the town with tank D12 in the lead and tank D14 following at 100 yards to provide covering fire. D12 dashed through the streets and overtook and then destroyed a German command car. The tanks moved quickly to the other edge of town cutting off the enemy's escape route. After a second call for infantry help 120 POWs were gathered up. A search of the command car, houses and an abandoned roadblock turned up large quantities of *Panzerfausts*.[32] None of the deadly antitank weapons had been used. Correcty employed by the soldiers occupying the town the weapons could have halted and destroyed the two light tanks and possibly those of B Company which were not far behind. The following day Dog Company collected an additional 900 prisoners.[33]

American and British POWs cheered the columns forward. The former prisoners made up a smaller but happier parade than that of the German POWs. Besides, the collection of prisoners remained a dangerous business.

On the afternoon of April 12 a firefight in Grand Steinum resulted in 50 prisoners. But before the town could be cleared the battalion's B Company tanks and infantry were ordered to move out to Schickelsheim. The move had barely gotten under way when two of the three infantrymen assigned to walk the POWs to the rear were killed by snipers.[34]

It was on Friday the 13th, while collecting prisoners for transfer to the rear, that Major Benjamin discovered 200 Finnish political prisoners near Farsleben. The men leading the eastward advance had previously encountered Polish, Russian, British, and American POWs but the pitiful condition of the Finns tested even the strongest constitutions.

The Finns, along with former officers of the Yugoslav and Dutch armies, were prisoners from a concentration camp near Hanover. The train guards, perhaps fearing being overtaken by the rapid American advance, had loaded the prisoners into sixty-eight railroad cars for transport to the far side of the Elbe River. An argument between the trainmen caused the cars to be placed on a siding to await transport deeper into eastern Germany. That night the accompanying SS troops deserted, leaving twelve military guards and the train commander in charge. The next morning 200 prisoners escaped. Members of this group accidently encountered Major Benjamin.

Benjamin scouted the area and found the train, at which point the remaining guards surrendered. The tank crews passed out all their food and cigarettes to the laughing and crying prisoners. To their horror it was discovered that there were 2,500 men shoved into the boxcars. Additional food was collected from the surrounding farmsteads and quarters for the sickest, including sixty with typhus, were sought.[35]

One tank and six doughs were assigned to watch the train throughout the night in case the guards who had deserted returned. Sergeant Gross, commander of tank D12, and the infantry squad leader took the steps necessary to protect their charges in a countryside filled with armed German stragglers. An infantry reconnaissance squad was sent out to familiarize themselves with the surrounding terrain and to identify possible enemy concentrations. The internees appointed a camp leader and set up a guard system using 2,500 unarmed men in extremely poor physical condition. These combined efforts resulted in the apprehension of several uniformed German soldiers and three of the former SS guards disguised as civilians. As dusk was approaching, Benjamin received notice that 26 enemy soldiers and 2 officers located nearby would surrender to an officer. On the way to the surrender location several additional prisoners were returned to the train. On the following day the military government took responsibility of the train's occupants.

In action around Marienthal between April 12 and 14, the 743d's Assault Gun Platoon working with the 125th Cavalry Squadron (attached temporarily to the 30th Division) captured 3,000 prisoners, a chemical warfare plant, an airfield, a German prisoner of war camp with 3,000 political prisoners, and another camp for Allied prisoners containing 2,500 officers. Also taken was a Radio Berlin substation.[36] Meanwhile the battalion tanks and infantry continued searching the countryside flanking the advance route. Houses and woods were always approached with caution and the collection of prisoners continued.

For the battalion, death on the continent began on the beaches of France; it ended on the streets of Magdeburg.

The following Tuesday, April 17, all the line companies participated in the attack on Magdeburg. At the outset of the attack the battalion's Mortar Platoon fired over 300 rounds of smoke to screen the tanks moving through the early morning ground haze surrounding the town. Battalion tanks advanced over secondary roads bypassing the 88s covering the main highways. The battle began in earnest on the outskirts of town and continued block by block between the high, closely built structures.

Combat within a large town was not too dissimilar from fighting among the hedgerows. The impression was that of moving from one room to another, some smaller, some larger, some allowing distant views, others not. The groups of tanks and troops worked their way from one confined area or street to the next; there was no hint as to when the end would be encountered.

As the platoon of C Company tanks advanced up a street the eyes behind the periscopes searched buildings, windows, and gutted interiors for a betraying movement. In front, beside, and behind the tanks infantrymen dodged around and through the rubble, past smoking wrecks and enemy dead. Despite all the cautions and accumulated experience, the platoon was caught unawares by the woman who dashed into the street and grabbed up a discarded *Panzerfaust*. She fired at the tank nearest her. The round penetrated the soft-sided turret, killing the gunner, and wounding the tank commander and cannoneer. Twelve months of combat experience sent turrets whirling in unison on the target and, as the barrels roared, the woman disappeared.[37]

In other villages movements up separate streets had taught that it was always pertinent to know what was going on in the alleyways to the left and right of an advance. The B Company dozer tank turned and knocked down the wall beside it, allowing the tanks behind to break into a sidestreet. The movement had been a good one, born of experience, but in the process the accompanying doughs were temporarily left behind. The platoon leader dismounted from his tank and a sniper's bullet sent his body slumping to the ground.[38]

The attack resumed at 6:30 the following morning. Tank dozers knocked down more walls to allow passage between streets choked with debris and filled in huge bomb craters from the previous day's airstrike. Sometimes the tanks fighting in the narrow streets fired up to 12 rounds of HE to overcome a roadblock. By early afternoon of the 18th the last resistance ceased. Three thousand yards away flowed the Elbe River.

Perry "Cock" Kelly pulled the large red, white and black flag down from its pole in front of Magdeburg's military headquarters.[39] Although it was not immediately known, the gunner and tank commander were the battalion's last wartime deaths.

VII

85 Points

FOR INQUIRE, I PRAY YOU, OF BYGONE AGES,
AND CONSIDER WHAT THE FATHERS HAVE FOUND;
FOR WE ARE BUT OF YESTERDAY, AND KNOW NOTHING,
FOR OUR DAYS ON EARTH ARE A SHADOW.
WILL THEY NOT TEACH YOU, AND TELL YOU,
AND UTTER WORDS OUT OF THEIR UNDERSTANDING?

Job 8: 8,9

THE battalion assisted in administering the Allied military government in Magdeburg. The duties varied from gathering and distributing food stuffs to liberated allied POWs, to the processing of German soldiers and the collection of civilian firearms. All the while the battalion positions were continually receiving indiscriminate artillery and sniper fire from across the Elbe. On April 25 the battalion's fighting war was unofficially over and the administrative battle began in earnest in the fifteen towns under 743d management. Five days later Hitler committed suicide eighty miles to the northeast. The battalion kept its K-ration boxes close at hand, but hot meals were now regularly available. As the last days of spring passed, the battalion readapted itself to a garrison-like lifestyle accompanied by reveille, roll call, inspections and training exercises.

On May 7, 1945, at General Eisenhower's schoolhouse headquarters in Reims, France, General Alfred Jodl signed the unconditional surrender of the Third Reich. On May 8, the war was officially over. The German garrison at Dunkerque held out for one more day. Southwest of Omaha Beach, on the coast of Brittany, the garrisons of L'Orient and Saint-Nazaire surrendered on May 10.

Award ceremonies and the dating of nurses and Red Cross volunteers broke the tankers' everyday routine. Many tankers replaced the risks of battle by taking turns riding in a captured glider that was towed aloft behind whatever vehicle was available. The veterans felt, at least for the moment, to be invincible. It would seem that the mere fact of survival had instilled a sense of immunity from harm. A short while later the battalion was sent on police duty in the Harz Mountains, southwest of Magdeburg. At the end of May the battalion moved yet again to Plauen near the Czechoslovakian border where the surrender was still under way of some German soldiers.

The branches used for camouflage during the last days of battle were pulled off the tanks. Service Company torches cut off the brackets that had held the sandbags that had saved so many lives. The muzzles of O'Sussanah and King Cock were cleaned and covered in fenced yards where they were now parked in short neat rows.

Some men now began leaving for home. Eighty-five points were necessary for immediate departure. The points were accumulated by virtue of time in service, campaigns participated in, and awards. Men possessing 85 points were sent by train back across the countryside they had fought over to Paris, and south to Marseille and waiting troop ships. Along the way, stops were made at huge tent cities with names like Baltimore; many had been built by German labor.

At the end of the long voyage home battalion veterans were once again hit by "friendly" fire. The men arriving in New York were kept aboard their ships by striking dockworkers. On November 27, 1945, the 743d Tank Battalion was officially decommissioned not far from Camp Shank, New York, where they had embarked for Europe in November 1943.

The twelve months of nearly continuous combat in the undergunned, underarmored Shermans had exacted a terrific toll from the battalion. Since June 6 of the previous year the battalion suffered 141 killed, 22 missing, and 316 wounded. Taken together, the 479 casualties represented the battalion at nearly full strength, and did not include non-battle casualties. The battalion's three line companies employing the Sherman M4 lost 96 tanks, 65 of which burned. D Company lost an additional 15 light tanks, nearly all of which had also burned. It should be kept in mind that the battalion consisted of only 52 tanks. The medium and light tanks losses, totaling 111 vehicles, constituted two tanks lost per crew. The division level use of the Sherman M4 did not fare better. In the long run sheer numbers might provide an advantage, but the price for technical inferiority was tremendous. The Third Armored Division, which at times worked in the 743d's zones of advance, lost 780 tanks and suffered 3,371 casualties, 706 of which were MIAs, the equivalent of approximately 141 tank crews. Third Armored KIAs represented another 442 crews![1] The ability to build numerous M4s and fill them with men is perhaps one of the least known and poorly understood tragedies of the American military industry of the Second World War.

Colonel Duncan remained in service and would later teach others his battalion's lessons. John Roncevich remained in armor, retiring after fighting and being wounded in both Korea and Vietnam. Ashley Camp became a doctor of medicine. Harold Froberg and Don Mason returned to their farms and only recently accepted full-time retirements. Dr. Tarlowski returned to peacetime medicine and lives today in New Mexico. Harry Hansen serves as a member of the board for The Battle of Normandy Foundation. George Johnson has accepted the duties of secretary-organizer for the battalion's reunions which, until recently, were held every two years at Harold Froberg's farm Blue Waters, in Lindstrom, Minnesota.

The occupation rights first established at the Potsdam Conference in July and August 1945 were not relinquished until forty-five years later, when the four wartime allies signed the *Treaty on the Final Settlement with Respect to Germany* in Moscow on Wednesday, September 12, 1990. The reunification of Germany with Berlin as its seat of government was endorsed. The ratification of the 1990 treaty had been preceded on June 6 by an agreement with the former Soviet Union to repay the United States 674 million dollars of World War II Lend Lease debts.

Along the Norman coast the beaches of fifty years ago are well marked by signs indicating "la route du debarquement." By mid-June the veterans' tours have long since departed from Normandy. Unlike the other coastal regions of France, the tourist season in Normandy really begins in early June, then shifts as it has done for over 50 years from returning veterans and their families to caravanning vacationers.

Within the whole of the coastal area initially encompassed by Operation Overlord, the forgotten seaside villages of Omaha beach appear somber. The glittery bustle and noise, common to the other beach landing sites of June 1944, are strangely absent at Omaha. The rural, almost unkempt appearance of Vierville presents the face of tranquility and contentment, at peace with the past. The mercantile value of history would seem, thankfully, to have been overlooked here. In Vierville the grass growing against the high stone walls bordering the fields, presents a view much as it once appeared years ago. The few houses of Vierville are as private today as they were then, and the restaurant above the beach relies heavily on seasonal trade. The clifftops which at one time denied access to the attackers from below, are now fenced with double strands of rusty barbwire to warn away unwary visitors from the unstable embankments. Below the wire, remnants of German concrete emplacements cling to the eroding cliff sides. Descending the seawall, the narrow strip of rocky beach is quickly supplanted by hard-packed ocher-colored sand. In the surf the tourists' discarded plastic trash mimics the lifeless forms that rolled in the cold Channel water.

The high tide which once threatened to engulf 743d tanks still draws itself close against the sandy bluffs. Beneath the cold waters off Saint-Laurent-sur-Mer rest the unrecovered tanks of the 743d and 741st Tank Battalions.[2] In the evening, a cold wind blows over the cliff tops while to the west a sun silently sets.

Farther west still, under the spreading branches of shade trees that block the hot August midday sun, men, wives, children, and visitors gather around George Johnson standing atop a picnic table. The vigorous and lean Able Company veteran brings the crowd to order while announcements are read.

In 1942, while in Arizona for desert warfare training, the 743d drove their armor for scenes in the film *Sahara*, starring Humphrey Bogart. Upon completion of the film the battalion was invited to Yuma for a special pre-public screening. On the evening of the show half of A Company descended on a local bar where a member, returning from furlough in California, had recently been robbed and beaten. In the words of a participant "upon arrival the men moved that bar into the street." The close relationships first forged in 1942 have only gained in strength.

Later in the day the men gather into the neat erect lines of their respective companies. Every year the ranks are thinner and every other year, since 1957, Howard and Lucille Froberg have welcomed the battalion back to their farm of Blue Waters.

Among the farmers, administrators, truck drivers, doctors, and professional soldiers, the conversation invariably reverts—with incredible precision of memory—to friends, close calls, final calls, muddy river banks and the hard sandy wastes of a beach to remember.

During these reunions no visitor can escape noticing the shared physical characteristics of these veteran tankers. Many have a pronounced limp from hours and days braced upright against the jolts of a bucking turret. Many also wear hearing aids, not because of aging degeneration, but because of the damage done decades ago by the enormously loud blasts of their tanks' main guns. Many have developed a slight cough from being confined in clouds of acrid breach gases.

After two days the men disperse to be brought together again by the common experiences and shared goals of their youth and the knowledge that the banquet of peace is savored most by those who have fasted in the dungeons of war.

Endnotes

CHAPTER I

1. Alvin Tisland, interviewed January 23, 1992. See also *Move Out Verify, The Combat Story of the 743d Tank Battalion* (Frankfurt am Main: July 1945), p. 22. Hereafter referred to as *Verify*.
2. *Verify*, p. 19.
3. After Action Reports, June 1944, p. 5. Hereafter referred to as A.A.R.
4. Landing Diagram, Omaha Beach, Sector of 116th RCT, published in Charles Taylor, *Omaha Beachhead (6 June–13 June, 1944),(* Washington D.C. Historical Division, U.S. War Department, 1945), p. 31. Additional information can be found in G. A. Harrison. *Cross Channel Attack U.S. Army in World War II, European Theater of Operations* (Washington D.C. Historical Division, U.S. War Department, 1947). Harrison does not mention the 743d.
5. The light tank companies were not deemed suitable for the beach assault.
6. R. P. Hunnicut. *Sherman, A History of the American Medium Tank* (Novato, Calif.: Presidio Press, 1978), p. 424.
7. Taylor, *Omaha Beachhead*, p. 39. The DD tanks were used on June 6 under conditions exceeding their operating limits. These tanks would later prove effective in the Ruhr River crossing.
8. A.A.R., June 1944.
9. Baker was allocated to Dog Green on the right of the beachhead, Charlie to the left on Dog Red. *Verify*, p. 19; and Taylor, *Omaha Beachhead*, pp. 33, 42.
10. From an interview with Howard Froberg, Jerry Latimer and Ed Miller, August 3, 1991.
11. U.S. Army 1st Division Operations Journal (APO #1, U.S. Army G-3 Journal, Appendix V. Recorded onboard the USS *Ancon*, June 6, 1944. Reproduced in Cornelius Ryan. *The Longest Day, June 6, 1944* (New York: Simon and Schuster, 1959), pp. 214–215.
12. A.A.R., June 1944, p. 1.
13. Don Mason, interview recorded May 1992.
14. Taylor, *Omaha Beachhead*, p. 48.
15. Fawcett received the Silver Star for the actions taken on behalf of his crewmembers. A.A.R., June 1944, pp. 40–41, January 1945.
16. Harry Hansen, interview recorded January 1992.

17. In the confusion of the moment A Company had been landed on all the beaches except Charlie, Dog Green and Dog White.
18. Unknown to 1st Platoon was that the LCT with B Company's CO had been sunk offshore by enemy artillery. Taylor, *Omaha Beachhead*, p. 42.
19. George Johnson, interviewed August 3, 1991. The testimonies of 743d D-Day veterans stand in stark contrast to the generalized accounts that have so influenced subsequent histories. One such example is that of Colonel Paul W. Thompson who wrote that the tank dozers "played no important role in the proceedings." See "D-Day On Omaha Beach" *Infantry Journal* (June 1945), pp. 34–48.
20. For his actions on D-Day, Staff Sergeant, later Captain, Jenkins was awarded the Distinguished Service Cross. I would like to thank Mrs. Tena Jenkins for her correspondence and the documentation she has provided me.
21. See Chapter II, pp. 52–54.
22. Don Mason, op. cit.
23. Correspondence with the author, September 13, 1991.
24. *Verify*, p. 29.
25. Frank Lancaster, interview recorded February 24, 1991.
26. Taylor, *Omaha Beachhead*, p. 39.
27. Alvin Tisland, op. cit.
28. John Parsons in "Omaha Beach 30 Years Ago D-Day," *Daily Mail*, Charleston, West Virginia, Thursday June 6, 1974, p. 1B.
29. Taylor, *Omaha Beachhead*, p. 57.
30. Taylor, *Omaha Beachhead*, p. 58.
31. Taylor, *Omaha Beachhead*, pp. 77, 93.
32. Taylor, *Omaha Beachhead*, p. 63.
33. Taylor, *Omaha Beachhead*, pp. 59, 80.
34. Taylor, *Omaha Beachhead*, p. 67.
35. Taylor, *Omaha Beachhead*, p. 92.
36. Taylor, *Omaha Beachhead*, p. 40.
37. Ryan, *The Longest Day*, pp. 214–215.
38. Tisland, op. cit.
39. Taylor, *Omaha Beachhead*, p. 93.
40. Taylor, *Omaha Beachhead*, p. 81.
41. Taylor, *Omaha Beachhead*, p. 95.
42. Taylor, *Omaha Beachhead*, p. 93.
43. Taylor, *Omaha Beachhead*, p. 104.
44. Companies L, I, K, and E of the 116th Infantry, 29th Infantry Division, Taylor, *Omaha Beachhead*, pp. 58, 73.
45. Taylor, *Omaha Beachhead*, p. 81.
46. *Verify*, p. 20.
47. Ryan, *The Longest Day*, pp. 258–259.
48. A.A.R., June 1944, pp. 5, 7.
49. Ryan, *The Longest Day*, p. 199.
50. Taylor, *Omaha Beachhead*, p. 28.
51. The 3d Battalion, 116th Infantry.
52. Taylor, *Omaha Beachhead*, p. 82.
53. The 2d Battalion of the 116th Infantry, Taylor, *Omaha Beachhead*, p. 98.
54. Taylor, *Omaha Beachhead*, p. 104. To the south, in front of Colleville-sur-Mer, Company G, 2d Battalion of the 116th Infantry had started inland at 0900 through routes later used by other elements of the 116th. After reaching the heights the troops started attacking Colleville when they too were hit by naval barrages. Taylor, *Omaha Beachhead*, p. 98.
55. Taylor, *Omaha Beachhead*, p. 102.

56. Taylor, *Omaha Beachhead*, pp. 103, 106. Ernie Pyle, *Brave Men* (New York: Henry Holt and Company, 1944), p. 361.
57. Taylor, *Omaha Beachhead*, p. 106.
58. Taylor, *Omaha Beachhead*, p. 101.
59. By members of the 121st Combat Engineers Battalion; A.A.R., June 1944, p. 2.
60. Taylor, *Omaha Beachhead*, p. 105.
61. A.A.R., June 1944, pp. 2, 5, 7.
62. Taylor, *Omaha Beachhead*, p. 101.
63. The 116th Infantry Regiment, 29th Division.
64. A.A.R., June 1944, p. 7.
65. A.A.R., June 1944, p. 5.
66. A.A.R., June 1944, p. 2.
67. Taylor, *Omaha Beachhead*, p. 109.
68. Taylor, *Omaha Beachhead*, p. 116.
69. Taylor, *Omaha Beachhead*, p. 110.
70. Correspondence with the author, January 28, 1992.
71. Taylor, *Omaha Beachhead*, p. 122.
72. Taylor, *Omaha Beachhead*, p. 123. See also the account of Oberleutnant Fritz Ziegelmann concerning the capture of the U.S. V Corps' Operations Plan on June 7 and the actions of the 352 Infantry Division on June 6 and 7, 1944, based on extracts from the unit's telephone diary. National Archives Microfiche Publication M1035, Foreign Military Studies, B series Fiche 0610, B-0636; and 0375, B-0388.
73. A.A.R., June 1944, p. 1.
74. The period spelling of Pointe du Hoe will be used throughout rather than the current usage of Point du Hoc. An early and carefully detailed account of this action can be found in "Pointe du Hoe, 2d Ranger Battalion, 6 June 1944" *Small Unit Actions* (Washington D.C.: War Department, Historical Division, 1946), pp. 1–63.
75. Comprised of 1st Battalion 116th Infantry, 5th Ranger Battalion, and Companies A, B, C, of the 2d Rangers.
76. Taylor, *Omaha Beachhead*, p. 129.
77. 3d Battalion, 116th Infantry. This action was aided by 113 rounds from the British cruiser *Glasgow*.
78. 743d A Company tanks and the 1st Battalion, 116th Infantry.
79. Taylor, *Omaha Beachhead*, pp. 129–130.
80. John Shanafelt, interviewed March 1992.
81. Taylor, *Omaha Beachhead*, p. 136.
82. The Caumont action, coordinated with the 2d and 29th Divisions to the south, was broadly participated in by 1st Division 102d Cavalry Squadron with 3 battalions of tanks; the 743d, 745th and 747th. The 2d Armored Division was waiting in Corps reserve. Taylor, *Omaha Beachhead*, p. 150.
83. Taylor, *Omaha Beachhead*, pp. 150–151.
84. Taylor, *Omaha Beachhead*, p. 153.
85. Taylor, *Omaha Beachhead*, p. 161.
86. The mistake was made by troops of the 115th Regiment, 29th Infantry Division.
87. While attached to the 120th Infantry, 3d Battalion.
88. George Johnson, op. cit.
89. On July 6 Winston Churchill wrote that he was surprised that gas had not been used against the Normandy invasion force, and was certain that German forces were prepared for similar warfare by the Allies. See Martin Gilbert, *Winston Churchill, Road to Victory 1941–1945* (Boston: Houghton Mifflin Company, 1986), pp. 840–841.
90. George Johnson, op. cit.

CHAPTER II

1. R. P. Hunnicutt, *Sherman, A History of the American Medium Tank* (Novato, Calif.: Presidio Press, 1978), p. 360.
2. Hunnicutt, p. 122. The discussion I have presented here is a simplified overview of a very complex yet interesting issue. Hunnicutt has gone a long way towards identifying many of the problems associated with American tank development between 1940 and 1945. Hunnicutt's book on the Sherman is, and will remain, the definitive work on this tank.
3. Hunnicutt, pp. 538–545.
4. Frank Lancaster, interview recorded February 24, 1991.
5. For a complete discussion of flotation devices see Hunnicutt, pp. 422–431. For a brief yet concise overview of the development of Britain's armor from 1940 to 1944 see Major K. J. Macksey "Buildup for D-Day, Balance of Armour," *History of the Second World War*, 63, pp. 1746–1755.
6. Colonel Duncan had been "loaned" to 3d Armored to establish and run the DD training program.
7. This account is taken from a letter written February 15, 1988, by Colonel Duncan detailing this incident. Additional information was derived from a letter written by Bob Jarvis, December 21, 1989. Copies of both letters were kindly provided me by Howard and Lucille Froberg.
8. No disciplinary action was taken. Reviewing authorities declared the tragedy a training accident.
9. The decision on June 6 to launch the battalion's DD tanks close in to shore was taken by a naval officer in conjunction with Captain Elder of the 743d.
10. David Irving provides many insights into problems with Allied weapons and the behind the scenes responses, in *The War Between the Generals* (New York: Congdon and Lattes, Inc., 1981), pp. 184, 199–201. Also see Max Hastings, *Overlord, D-Day and the Battle for Normandy* (New York: Simon and Schuster, 1984), pp. 186–187.
11. These two articles are unusual in that they are earlier than the majority of reports and also that they appeared in the monthly *Science News Letter*. Wartime censorship of the press was vague from the time President Roosevelt declared a state of emergency on September 2, 1939, through to the end of hostilities. Guidelines for the press were covered in a pamphlet entitled *Codes of Wartime Practices for Press and Radio*. First issued on January 15, 1942, this pamphlet went through several editions. The security concern was stated as those "subjects which contained information of value to the enemy" (pp. 6, 33-36). Tanks were listed under restrictions on reporting details of the production of vehicles of war (p. 4 in the 1942 edition; and p. 5 in the February 1, 1943, edition). Some clarification of the censorship material was provided by the December 1, 1943, edition censoring reports on the progress of production for general categories of war materiel. Within this edition tanks could be reported on but statistical information was to be avoided (pp. 4–5).
12. Milo Ryan, *History in Sound, A Descriptive Listing of the Kiro-CBS Collection of Broadcasts of the World War II Years and After in the Phonoarchive of the University of Washington* (Seattle: University of Washington Press, 1963), No. 3072.
13. Ryan, No. 3112.
14. Ryan, No. 3126.
15. For a brief overview of the British counterpart to this same problem see Hastings, *Overlord*, pp. 194–195.
16. Irving, *The War*, p. 184.
17. Hunnicutt, p. 212.
18. L. Israel, ed. *The State of the Union Messages of the Presidents. 1790–1966*, III (New York: Chelsea House, Robert Hector Publisher, 1966), p. 2888.

19. Hanson Baldwin, "American Tanks," I, II, III, *New York Times,* March 18, 19, 20, 1945.

20. Baldwin, "The German Blow," III "New German Tanks Proved Superior to Ours-Inquiry by Congress Urged," *New York Times,* January 5, 1945.

21. Paynter Gask, *Newsweek,* February 26, 1945, "Must We Defeat Germany With Inferior Weapons?" p. 38. Also "Chasing the Tiger," *Newsweek* 25:33, March 19, 1945, pp. 33–34, and "Driblets of Tanks," *Newsweek* 25:37, March 26, 1945, p. 37.

22. *Newsweek,* January 15, 1945, pp. 26–27, "Decision to the Tiger," and "Doubt on Caliber of U.S. Arms Raised by New German Weapons."

23. Ernest Leiser, "Shells Bounce Off Tigers, Veteran U.S. Tankmen Say," *Stars and Stripes,* February 23, 1945.

24. *Life,* "The Battle of the Tanks," pp. 41–42, March 26, 1945.

25. Hunnicutt, p. 310.

26. Author's emphasis. This final demonstration occurred on June 12, 1944 (Hunnicutt, ibid.). Perhaps Patton was already rethinking his earlier commitment to the 75 mm.

27. Joel Matteson (Captain, A Company) indicated that battlefield tactics were kept simple and were most often of the moment. Correspondence with the author September 1, 1990.

28. Hunnicutt, p. 213. An anachronistic yet interesting comparison is the current army light tank, the Sheridan M-551A1. Used in Vietnam it was also airdropped into Panama during Operation Just Cause. The Sheridan carries a 152 mm main gun, a cupola mounted .50 cal. M-2 heavy machine gun and a coaxially mounted 7.62 mm M-60 light machine gun. Konrad F. Schreier, Jr.'s suggestion that the Sherman tank is the only WWII tank still in service is left unqualified by the author in "U.S. Army Tank Development 1925–1940," *Armor* (May–June 1990), pp. 24–29.

29. John Shanafelt, interview recorded March 12, 1992.

30. Hunnicutt, p. 206.

31. Alvin Tisland, interviewed January 23, 1992.

32. As far as I am aware, the real scope of this problem has never been investigated. In studying the After Action Reports of the 743d the number of M.I.A.'s (that is those crew members lost in such incidents) dropped dramatically but was never totally prevented after the battalion introduced sandbagging during the Normandy campaign.

33. Howard Froberg, interviewed August 3, 1991. The Sherman was so well known for its combustibility that German tankers nicknamed it the "Ronson," after their cigarette lighter, whereas the British—less than affectionately—dubbed it the "Tommy cooker." Hastings, p. 191.

34. Hunnicutt, p. 152.

35. Ibid.

36. Harlan Whitcomb, interview recorded January 23, 1991.

37. William L. Shirer. *The Collapse of the Third Republic, An Inquiry into the Fall of France in 1940* (New York: Simon and Schuster, 1969). For a full discussion of the problems and questions surrounding the Allied and German tank question early in the war, see pp. 611–624.

38. The British Matilda was better armored and its 2 pounder could outperform the primary German fighting tank of the period, the German Mark III. See Major General F. W. von Mellenthin, *Panzer Battles, A Study of the Employment of Armor in the Second World War* (London: Casell & Co. Ltd., 1956, rpt., 1983), p. 12.

39. Von Mellenthin, p. 54.

40. Von Mellenthin, pp. 54–55, n. 17, 18.

41. For the allied response to the African armored experience see Colonel H. C. B. Rogers, *Tanks in Battle* (London: Seeley Service and Co., 1965), particularly pages 171; and pp. 184–185. The author provides a detailed comparison of all Allied and German tanks in the appendix, pp. 231–233.
42. Hunnicutt, pp. 195, 198. See also Konrad F. Scheier, Jr. "U.S. Army Tank Development 1925–1940," *Armor* (May–June 1990), p. 29.
43. Hunnicutt, pp. 219–220.
44. Hunnicutt, p. 220.
45. Hunnicutt, p. 212.
46. Ibid.
47. No really new tank became available to the army until 1959 with the introduction of the M-60 which like its predecessors was kept in long service through into the 1980s by the same model improvement techniques applied to the Sherman. For a full discussion of American tank development and acquisition processes see Orr Kelly, *King of the Killing Zone, The Story of the M-1, America's Super Tank* (New York: Berkley Books, 1989), pp. 13–43.
48. "The Tanks Are O.K." *Time*, February 12, 1945. p. 17.
49. Wes Gallagher, "Driblets of Tanks," *Newsweek*, March 26, 1945, p. 37.
50. Tisland, op. cit.

CHAPTER III

1. Perry Kelly, interviewed January 16, 1992.
2. Joel Matteson correspondence with the author May 9, 1991.
3. "Green Death" was first used as a title in Part II, in *Move Out Verify*.
4. A.A.R., August 1944, p. 1.
5. *Verify*, p. 55.
6. Ibid.
7. Matteson, op. cit.
8. It is interesting to compare the track width of the Sherman at thirty-two tons with that of the Panther at 26" and the 56-ton Tiger's 28.5" wide track.
9. *Verify*, p. 50.
10. A.A.R., July 1944, p. 1.
11. *Verify*, p. 51.
12. *Verify*, p. 55.
13. Robert L. Hewitt. *Work Horse of the Western Front, The Story of the 30th Infantry Division* (Washington: Infantry Journal Press, 1946), pp. 28–29.
14. Dr. Ashley Camp, interview recorded April 15, 1991.
15. Hewitt, p. 29.
16. They were replaced later in the day by a platoon of C Company tanks. A.A.R. July 1944, p. 3.
17. Hewitt, p. 29.
18. Hewitt, p. 30.
19. Hewitt, pp. 30–31.
20. 2d Battalion 117th Infantry.
21. From correspondence with the author January 28, 1992.
22. From the French *de trier* "to sort."
23. Dr. Carl Tarlowski, interviewed in *Hahnemann University: Medicine and War*, Spring, 1992, pp. 18–19.
24. *Verify*, p. 56.
25. A.A.R., July 1944, p. 6.
26. A.A.R., July 1944, p. 4.
27. A.A.R., August 1944, p. 4.
28. Principally the 14th Parachute Regiment, 5th Parachute Division. *Verify*, p. 60; Hewitt, p. 31.

29. A.A.R., July 1944, p. 5.
30. John Shanafelt, interview recorded March 1992.
31. Harlan Whitcomb, interview recorded January 24, 1991.
32. Whitcomb, op. cit.
33. Correspondence with the author, dated September 1, 1990.
34. *Verify*, p. 56.
35. In support of the 120th Infantry.
36. Hewitt, p. 37.
37. Hewitt, pp. 40–43.
38. George Johnson, interview recorded August 3, 1991.
39. A.A.R., July 1944, p. 6.
40. Whitcomb, op. cit.
41. Harry Hansen, interview recorded January 1992; Whitcomb, and A.A.R., July 1944, p. 7.
42. Hans Speidel, *Invasion 1944: Rommel and the Normandy Campaign* (Chicago: Henry Regnery Company, 1950), pp. 115–116.
43. Hewitt, pp. 48–49.
44. Gathered for the attack was 1st SS Panzer Division *Leibstandarte Adolf Hitler*, 2d SS Panzer Division *Das Reich* with the 17th SS Panzer Grenadier Division *Goetz von Berlichingen*, the 2d Panzer Division and the 116th Panzer Division.
45. *Verify*, p. 72.
46. 30th Division's 120th Infantry's 2d Battalion.
47. A.A.R., August 1944, p. 2.
48. John Shanafelt. See also *Verify*, pp. 74–75.
49. A.A.R., August 1944, p. 2.
50. A.A.R., August 1944, p. 3.
51. Speidel, p. 132.
52. Correspondence with the author, June 6, 1991.

CHAPTER IV

1. At this time the 743d was part of a task force established by Brigadier General Harrison. This highly mobile force also consisted of the 125th Cavalry Squadron, the 30th Reconnaissance Troop; the 1st Battalion, 119th Infantry; the 118th Field Artillery Battalion; Company A, 105th Engineer Battalion; and Company A, 823d Tank Destroyer Battalion. See Hewitt, pp. 86–88.
2. *Verify*, p. 84.
3. This individual was the main character named Andre in *B Is For Barbara*, a fictionalized account of the 743d written by battalion veteran Wayne Robinson. Attempts to locate "Andre" have proved fruitless, despite assistance sought through various French sources.
4. Hewitt, p. 99.
5. 1st Battalion 117th Infantry. *Verify*, p. 90.
6. See for example Guenther Blumentritt, *Von Rundstedt: The Soldier and the Man*, Cuthbert Reavely, trans. (London: Odhams Press Ltd., 1952), pp. 260–264.
7. A useful introductory overview to the construction and distribution of the West Wall defenses can be found in Keith Mallory's and Arvid Ottar's *The Architecture of War* (New York: Pantheon Books, 1973), pp. 108–123.
8. *Verify*, pp. 96–97.
9. Hewitt, pp. 100–130. *Verify*, pp. 97–100.
10. A.A.R., October 1944, p. 9.
11. Many of the groups battling the 30th and 743d were those encountered later during the Battle of Mortain. The 116th Panzer Division arrived from Arnhem, and the 1st SS Panzer Division moved up from Trier near the German-Luxembourg border. See Hewitt, pp. 135–137.

12. Hewitt, p. 134; See also MacDonald. *The Siegfried Line Campaign* (Washington D.C.: Department of the Army, 1963), p. 301. Beiber was awarded the Distinguished Service Cross for this action on February 9, 1945.
13. This occurred October 7 while supporting 3d Battalion 117th Infantry Regiment. A.A.R., October 1944, p. 9.
14. A.A.R., October 1944, p. 11.
15. This occurred on October 10, A.A.R., October 1944, p. 11. Kirksey received the Distinguished Service Cross on February 9, 1945.
16. *Verify*, pp. 99–100. It is difficult to understand MacDonald's remark regarding the sensibility of the choice of the Sherman M4 as the Americans' tank judged solely on its use and performance during the Siegfried Line Campaign. Infantry advances depended heavily upon battalion-level tank support, and the many instances of heroism while using this tank do not dispell nor offset its numerous shortcomings. See MacDonald, pp. 620–621.
17. MacDonald, p. 303.
18. Hewitt, pp. 136–140.
19. The Wurselen defenders were overrun in Linden before they could regroup. Hewitt, p. 149.
20. *Verify*, p. 110.
21. MacDonald, p. 558; also see Hewitt, p. 162, and pp. 144–165.
22. The attack had started with the 120th's 2d Battalion, then the 1st, then the 3d, which was then followed up by the 2d and 3d.
23. *Verify*, p. 114. During interviews battalion veterans recalled that they avoided the use of colored rear deck panels for this very reason.
24. MacDonald, p. 616.
25. Joel Matteson, correspondence with the author, May 9, 1991. Also see Hunnicut, pp. 214–216.
26. A.A.R., December 1944, p. 8.
27. A.A.R., December 1944, p. 12.
28. Harlan Whitcomb, interview recorded January 24, 1991.
29. A.A.R., December 1944, p. 16.
30. Captain John Roncevich, interviewed March 1992.
31. This excerpt is from a personal account of the Bulge campaign written by 1st Lt. Joseph A. Couri, Platoon Leader 2d Platoon, Company A. My thanks to Mrs. Majorie McCullough who provided me a copy of this work.
32. The importance of this battle was already being registered in publication the same year. See for example Sergeant Theodore Draper, "Battle in the Bulge," *Infantry Journal*, May 1945, pp. 8-17.
33. These were the 28th and 4th Infantry Divisions, both needing approximately 3,400 replacements. They were joined by the 106th Infantry Division. In reserve was a combat command of the 9th Armored Division. See MacDonald, pp. 614–615.
34. Couri, op. cit.
35. A.A.R., December 1944, p. 19.
36. I would like to thank Lucille Froberg for her permission to quote from her unpublished manuscript *Coincidences* (1984).
37. A.A.R., December 1944, p. 18.
38. A.A.R., December 1944, p. 19.
39. I Company, 119th Infantry, was positioned outside the town, with L Company, 119th Infantry Regiment, inside the town. Also see Charles B. MacDonald, *A Time For Trumpets: The Untold Story of the Battle of the Bulge* (New York: William Morrow and Company, 1985), pp. 438–441; and John S. D. Eisenhower, *The Bitter Woods* (New York: G. P. Putnam's Sons, 1969), pp. 261–262, 266, 279. Napier Crookenden's *The Battle of the Bulge, 1944* (New York: Charles

Scribner's Sons, 1980) concentrated on the southern half of the Bulge center-
ing on Bastogne.

40. Whitcomb, op. cit.
41. A.A.R., December 1944, pp. 21–23; and Hewitt, pp. 182–183.
42. A.A.R., December 1944, p. 21.
43. Couri, op. cit. Gas Dump No. 2 contained 2,110,920 gallons of gas and was
    located 1 to 2 miles from Spa. Gas Dump No. 3 contained 997,730 gallons of
    gas and was located between Francorchamps and Stavelot. See Hewitt, p. 173.
44. Couri, op. cit.
45. Couri, op. cit.
46. Whitcomb, op. cit.
47. Matteson correspondence with the author dated June 4, 1991. Also see A.A.R.,
    December 1944, p. 21.
48. A.A.R., December 1944, p. 24.
49. Recounted in a letter by Earl Dhanse to Charles Brown dated July 26, 1987.
50. A.A.R., December 1944, p. 25.
51. A.A.R., December 1944, pp. 28–29.
52. Following one mission of 480 rounds four men had to be revived and one sent
    to the hospital. A.A.R., January 1945, p. 13.
53. A.A.R., December 1944, pp. 26–27.
54. Couri, op. cit.
55. Froberg, op. cit.
56. Tisland, interviewed January 23, 1992.
57. A.A.R., December 1944, p. 29.
58. A.A.R., December 1944, p. 30.
59. The incident was never forgotten, neither by Howard Froberg nor Anny Maertins
    de Noordhout. In 1983 the Frobergs received a letter from Anny that was later
    published in the *30th Division News*. From this, Battalion veteran Richard
    Threadgould determined that the baby Monique lives today in Stavelot.
60. Tom Snyder, interviewed August 4, 1991.
61. A.A.R., December 1944, p. 35.
62. A.A.R., January 1945, p. 2.
63. From a letter written by Wayne Robinson to Charles Brown dated November
    19, 1985.
64. A.A.R., January 1945, p. 3.
65. Couri, op. cit.
66. A.A.R., January 1945, p. 26.
67. Perry Kelly, interviewed January 16, 1992.
68. Dr. Ashley Camp, interview recorded April 15, 1991.
69. Hewitt, pp. 200–202; and A.A.R., January 1945, p. 21.
70. Whitcomb, op. cit.
71. Action conducted alongside the 2d Battalion, 117th Infantry regiment.
72. A.A.R., January 1945, p. 29.
73. A.A.R., January 1945, p. 31.
74. A.A.R., January 1945, p. 31.
75. Hewitt, p. 206.
76. A.A.R., January 1945, p. 32.
77. A.A.R., January 1945, pp. 32-33. During the January Bulge action the battal-
    ion lost 2 medium tanks, 4 light tanks and one half-track. Six men were killed
    and 18 wounded. During the same period the battalion destroyed 10 Mark IVs
    and captured 4, knocked out 2 Mark Vs and 2 half-tracks, 6 AT guns and 9
    horse-drawn sleighs.

CHAPTER V

1. *Verify*, p. 149.
2. A.A.R., February 1945, pp. 1–2.
3. Hewitt, p. 5, and A.A.R., February 1945, p. 3.
4. A.A.R., February 1945, p. 7.
5. A.A.R., February 1945, p. 8. For information on the Roer River dams and attempts to wrest their control from the Germans see Charles B. MacDonald *The Last Offensive* (Washington, D.C.: U.S. Army, 1973), pp. 70–83.
6. These were the first upgraded M4s received since before the Bulge. A.A.R., February 1945, p. 10.
7. Although the profile was little changed from the 75 mm M4, the long-barreled tanks were shown to the 120th Infantry Regiment so that the doughs could familiarize themselves with the new model. Later, some of the tanker's excitement was dampened when a bogie wheel broke on a subsequent visit-demonstration to the 117th Infantry Regiment. A minor affair but a major headache when Service Company discovered there were no manuals available describing the removal and replacement of the wheel. A.A.R., February 1945, p. 12.
8. A.A.R., February 1945, p. 15.
9. Hewitt, pp. 214–215. Despite these precautions when the 743d passed through Aachen heading back north Axis Sally broadcasted a greeting to the 743d she nicknamed "Roosevelt's SS."
10. Hewitt, p. 215.
11. Hewitt, pp. 215–216. On the importance of Operation Grenade see MacDonald *The Last Offensive*, pp. 135–162 and 170–171.
12. Hewitt, p. 212.
13. The 82d Smoke Generator Company maintained the smoke cover for 32 hours. Hewitt, p. 221.
14. *Verify*, p. 147.
15. A.A.R., February 1945, p. 17.
16. Hewitt, pp. 216, 221.
17. Attacking alongside 117th Infantry. A.A.R., February 1945, p. 19.
18. A.A.R., February 1945, p. 19.
19. A.A.R., February 1945, p. 20.
20. F Company 117th Infantry Regiment.
21. Account provided to the author by Bob Anderson, August 4, 1991.
22. A.A.R., February 1945, p. 20. MacDonald, *The Last Offensive*, pp. 166–167.
23. A.A.R., February 1945, p. 19.
24. A.A.R., February 1945, p. 18.
25. Crookenden suggests that some Panthers used in the Bulge offensive were already equipped with infrared gun sights (*Battle of the Bulge*, p. 45). Although experiments were already under way with infrared equipment it would be decades before practical night vision devices were available. See Hunnicutt, pp. 256, 400. Sometimes searchlights were played on the cloud cover to transform the battlefield darkness into twilight. See MacDonald, *The Last Offensive*, p. 156 and n. 35.
26. *Verify*, pp. 114–115.
27. 1st Battalion, 117th Infantry Regiment. These operations later became the subject of an article written by Colonel Duncan while teaching at the Command and General Staff College. See Colonel William Duncan, "Tanks and Infantry in Night Attacks," *Military Review* (1948), pp. 46–56.
28. Duncan, p. 52.
29. "A" Squadron, 1st Lothian and Border Yeomanry.
30. A.A.R., February 1945, pp. 23–24. This attack was made in conjunction with the 120th Infantry Regiment supported by the 744th Tank Battalion advancing on the villages of Kalrath and Grottherten.

31. A.A.R., February 1945, p. 22.
32. Duncan, pp. 54–55.
33. A.A.R., February 1945, p. 24.
34. Perry Kelly interviewed January 16, 1992.
35. Duncan, p. 49.

CHAPTER VI

1. *Verify*, p. 169.
2. A.A.R., March 1945, p. 1.
3. A.A.R., March 1945, p. 2.
4. A.A.R., March 1945, p. 8.
5. A.A.R., March 1945, pp. 5–6.
6. A.A.R., March 1945, p. 7.
7. A.A.R., March 1945, p. 10.
8. A.A.R., March 1945, p. 13.
9. A.A.R., March 1945, p. 12.
10. For a complete overview of the Rhine River crossings and their objectives see MacDonald, *The Last Offensive*, pp. 303–308.
11. A.A.R., March 1945, p. 12.
12. Ibid.
13. 1st and 3d Battalion, 117th Infantry Regiment.
14. 2d Battalion, 117th Infantry.
15. A.A.R., March 1945, p. 16. Also see MacDonald, ibid., pp. 315–317.
16. A.A.R., March 1945, pp. 15–16.
17. A.A.R., March 1945, p. 16.
18. A.A.R., March 1945, p. 17.
19. A.A.R., April 1945, p. 1.
20. A.A.R., April 1945, p. 2.
21. John Roncevich, interviewed March 1992.
22. A.A.R., April 1945, pp. 3–4.
23. The tanks were accompanying the 1st Battalion, 120th Infantry Regiment.
24. A.A.R., April 1945, p. 5.
25. A.A.R., April 1945, pp. 5–6.
26. A.A.R., April 1945, p. 7.
27. A.A.R., April 1945, pp. 7, 9–10.
28. A.A.R., April 1945, p. 11.
29. A.A.R., April 1945, pp. 12–13.
30. A.A.R., April 1945, p. 14.
31. A.A.R., April 1945, pp. 13–14.
32. A.A.R., April 1945, p. 15.
33. A.A.R., April 1945, p. 16.
34. A.A.R., April 1945, p. 14.
35. A.A.R., April 1945, pp. 16–19.
36. A.A.R., April 1945, p. 19.
37. Ashley Camp, interview recorded April 15, 1991.
38. A.A.R., April, 1945, pp. 20–24.
39. Kelly's prized souvenir remains in his possession.

CHAPTER VII

1. *Spearhead in the West, 1941–45: The Third Armored Division* (Frankfurt am Main: Third Armored Division, 1945). The casualty figures cited here are from June 29, 1944, through April 22, 1945 (p. 253).
2. No attempt has ever been made to recover these tanks. See Alan Weiner, "The First Wave," *American Heritage Magazine* (May/June 1987).

Index

66th Air Ground Forces Dance Band, 68
82d Smoke Generator Company, 139 n13
102d Cavalry Squadron, 132 n82
105th Engineer Battalion, 136 n1
118th Field Artillery Battalion, 136 n1
125th Cavalry Squadron, 123, 136 n1
230th Field Artillery Battalion, 105
743d Tank Battalion, "Verify", A Company, 2, 3, 4, 7, 8, 9, 10, 12, 14, 16, 17, 18, 22, 23, 26, 27, 42, 45, 46, 48, 51, 52, 56, 57, 58, 61, 63, 65, 67, 70, 75, 76, 77, 82, 86, 87, 88, 92, 93, 94, 95, 96, 97, 99, 100, 102, 103, 106, 121, 128; 743d Assault Gun Platoon, 26, 38, 41, 55, 66, 70, 73, 74, 75, 79, 87, 88, 91, 93, 94, 95, 101, 102, 103, 105, 123, and Time On Targets (TOTs), 93; 743d B Company, 2, 3, 4, 6, 8, 10, 13, 15, 16, 17, 19, 22, 26, 27, 41, 42, 43, 44, 46, 52, 56, 57, 64, 67, 70, 73, 75, 78, 80, 82, 83, 86, 87, 88, 89, 92, 94, 95, 97, 102, 103, 105, 106, 121, 123; 743d C Company, 1, 2, 3, 4, 7, 8, 12, 13, 15, 16, 17, 20, 21, 22, 26, 27, 36, 42, 48, 51, 52, 54, 56, 57, 61, 63, 67, 70, 73, 74, 75, 84, 86, 87, 92, 95, 96, 97, 103, 105, 106, 123; 743d D Company, 26, 50, 51, 56, 68, 73, 88, 103, 106, 121, 122, and Omaha Beach landings, 130 n5; 743d Headquarters Company, 5, 12, 16, 19, 22, 38, 45, 48, 66, 70, 83, 95,
100, 105, and air-ground liaison, 94, 95, 100, 102; 743d Mortar Platoon, 26, 42, 79, 94, 95, 123, and infantry support, 26, 94, 95; 743d Service Company, 23, 45, 47, 67, 85, 100, 126, 139 n7
823d Tank Destroyer Battalion, 85, 95, 136 n1

A

Aachen, 61, 62, 63, 64, 65, 66, 68, 90
Aachen Gap, 65, 66
Aberdeen Proving Grounds, Maryland, 26, 95
Alsdorf, 63
Altdorf, 95
Ambleve River, 80, 81
American Armored Divisions: 2d Armored Division, 51, 63, 98, 104, 105, 106, 132 n82; 3d Armored Division, 44, 45, 76, 82, 127; 7th Armored Division, 88; 8th Armored Division, 104; 9th Armored Division, 137 n33
Anderson, Robert, 94
Antwerp, 61
Ardennes, 26, 30, 36, 61, 62, 69, 70, 91, 94, 103
Army Ground Forces, 29, 35
Arnhem, 63
Articles of War, 91
Atlantic Wall, 62
Avranches, 21, 54

Index

Index

8, 12; Easy Green, 2, 3, 7, 12, 16; Easy Red, 2, 6, 12; Fox Green, 2, 14; Fox Red, 2, 16; Landing Craft Man (LCM), 27, and amphibious tank training, 9; naval support on Omaha, Carmick, 14; Texas, 14; Ellyson, 20; Glasgow, 132 n77
"Operation Grenade," the Roer River crossing, 90, 91. *See also* Roer River
Orr Emmels, 88
Ottre, 88, 89

P

Panzerfaust, 39, 45, 51, 105, 121, 123
Parfondruy, 81
Paris, 60, 126
Parsons, John, 12
Pattern, 67, 70
Patton, George, 25, 32, 58, 59
Paynter, Henry, 31
Peiper, Colonel Joachim, 71, 73, 76, 82
Philips, Vodra, 8, 10
Plain of Cologne, 90, 98
Plauen, 126
Plymouth, England, 28
Pointe-du-Hoe, 19, 20
Pont, 86
Pont-du-Saint-Fromond, 41, 42, 44
Pont-Hebert, 45
Potsdam Conference, 127
Preble, George, 101
Putz, 97

R

Ranger Battalions: 2d Ranger Battalion, 12; 5th Ranger Battalion, 12, 13, 20
Recht, 86
Reichsautobahn, 90
Reims, 125
Remagen, 101
Remonchamps, 75
Rhine River, 90, 98, 101, 102, 105
Riegel mine, 93
Rimberg, 63
Roanne, 75, 77, 79
Robinson, Wayne, 83
Roer River, 62, 66, 67, 68, 70, 84, 88, 89, 90, 91, 92, 94, 95, 98, 100, 102
Roer River dams, 90, 91
Romagny, 56, 57
Rommel, Field Marshal Erwin, 53
Roncevich, John, 104, 127

Roosevelt, Franklin D., 15, 30, 36
Roosevelt's SS, 139 n9
Ruhr, 98
Ruhr region, 36, 101
Ruy, 75

S

S-mines, 93
Saint-Barthelemy, 55
Saint-Fromond and Airel, 41, 42
Saint-Jean-de-Daye, 36, 42, 43
Saint-Laurent-sur-Mer, 14, 15, 18, 19
Saint-Lo, 21, 49, 54
Saint-Nazaire, 126
Saint-Pierre-du-Mont, 19, 20
Saint-Romphire, 53
Saint-Samson Bon Fosse, 53
Saint-Vith, 85, 86, 87, 88
Sart-Lez-Saint-Vith, 86
Schanzenberg, 102
Scherpenseel, 61
Schickelsheim, 122
Schlommofurth, 86
Schuh mine, 93
Screaming Meemies. *See Nebelwerfer*
Sée River, 54, 55
Seine River, 60
Shanafelt, John, 32, 33, 56, 57
Sherman M4A1 Medium tank: amphibious operations, 1–16; armament of, 26, 31, 34. *See also* M4A1, M4A2, M4A3E2; casualties with, 27, 34; Breach gases, and Sherman M4, 80, 138 n52; Sherman M4, and reorganization due to tank losses, 48; and battlefield promotions due to casualties, 48; comparison of track widths with German Panther and Tiger tanks, 31, 135 n8; congressional investigation of 30; dozer tanks, 12, 14, 17, 22; duckbill extensions, 41, 67; flammability, 31, 33, 40, 44, 57; gyro-stabilizers, 67; ice cleats, 85; Little Joe, 79; night vision, 139 n25; night operations, 95, significance of, 98; radios, 47; radio secrecy, 47; sandbagging, 49, 67, 87, 91, 100, 134 n32; wartime censorhip, 133 n11
Sherman M4A1, 26
Sherman M4A2, 26, 33
Sherman M4A3E2, 26, 91
Shophaven, 92
Siegfried Line Campaign, 36, 83, 95

Index